fat-free
Italian
kitchen

ANNE SHEASBY

fat-free
Italian
kitchen

80 healthy recipes, full of mediterranean zest

southwater

This edition is published by Southwater

Distributed in the UK by
The Manning Partnership
251-253 London Road East
Batheaston
Bath BA1 7RL
tel. 01225 852 727
fax 01225 852 852

Distributed in Canada by
General Publishing
895 Don Mills Road
400–402 Park Centre
Toronto, Ontario M3C 1W3
tel. 416 445 3333
fax 416 445 5991

Published in the USA by
Anness Publishing Inc.
27 West 20th Street
Suite 504
New York
NY 10011
fax 212 807 6813

Distributed in Australia by
Sandstone Publishing
Unit 1, 360 Norton Street
Leichhardt
New South Wales 2040
tel. 02 9560 7888
fax 02 9560 7488

Southwater is an imprint of Anness Publishing Limited
Hermes House, 88–89 Blackfriars Road, London SE1 8HA
tel. 020 7401 2077; fax 020 7633 9499

© Anness Publishing Limited 2001

Publisher Joanna Lorenz
Managing Editor Judith Simons
Project Editor Mariano Kälfors
Consultant Editor Anne Sheasby
Jacket Design The Bridgewater Book Company Limited
Nutritional Analysis Jill Scott
Recipes Catherine Atkinson, Carla Capalbo, Kit Chan, Jacqueline Clarke, Maxine Clarke, Frances Cleary, Carol Clements, Roz Denny, Matthew Drennan, Joanna Farrow, Christine France, Sarah Gates, Shirley Gill, Carole Handslip, Christine Ingram, Patricia Lousada, Norma MacMillan, Sue Maggs, Elizabeth Martin, Sarah Maxwell, Janice Murfitt, Annie Nichols, Angela Nilsen, Maggie Pannell, Louise Pickford, Jennie Shapter, Anne Sheasby, Hilaire Walden, Laura Washburn, Steven Wheeler, Kate Whiteman, Judy Williams, Elizabeth Wolf-Cohen, Jeni Wright
Photographers: Karl Adamson, Edward Allwright, David Armstrong, Steve Baxter, Nicki Dowey, James Duncan, Michelle Garrett, Amanda Heywood, David Jordan, Dave King, Don Last, William Lingwood, Patrick McLeavey, Michael Michaels, Thomas Odulate, Peter Reilly
Designers Nigel Partridge, Ian Sandom
Editorial Reader Richard McGinlay
Production Controller Yolande Denny

Previously published as part of a larger compendium, *Fat-Free Italian Cooking*.

1 3 5 7 9 10 8 6 4 2

• Bracketed terms are intended for American readers
• For all recipes, quantities are given in both metric and imperial measures, and, where appropriate, measures are also given in standard cups and spoons. Follow one set, but not a mixture, because they are not interchangeable.
• Standard spoon and cup measurements are level.
1 tsp = 5ml, 1 tbsp = 15ml, 1 cup = 250ml/8fl oz
• Australian standard tablespoons are 20ml. Australian readers should use 3 tsp in place of 1 tbsp for measuring small quantities of gelatine, flour, salt etc.
• Medium (US large) eggs are used unless otherwise stated.

PUBLISHER'S NOTE
The nutritional analysis of recipes excludes all optional items and serving suggestions.

CONTENTS

INTRODUCTION

Italians are passionate about their food and always enjoy spending time preparing, cooking and eating food with family and friends. Food is one of their greatest pleasures and Italians are fortunate to be able to enjoy many regional variations in the dishes they eat. Italian food is thought by many of us to be laden with calories and fat, but in fact an appealing scope and variety of flavours from Italy can be enjoyed as part of a healthy, low-fat diet.

Many traditional Italian foods, such as the abundance of fresh Mediterranean sun-ripened vegetables, fresh herbs and many different types of pasta are naturally low in fat, making them ideal to enjoy as part of a low-fat eating plan. Quality and freshness of foods are both of great importance to the Italians and much of the fresh produce eaten in Italy is grown or produced locally. When it comes to cooking foods such as vegetables, they are often prepared in simple ways to bring out their delicious and natural flavours.

Olive oil is the primary fat used for cooking in Italy and it is also commonly used for dressing foods such as salads. Olive oil is a "healthier" type of fat that is high in monounsaturated fat and low in saturated fat and so long as it is used in moderation, it can also be enjoyed as part of a low-fat diet.

Some other typical Italian ingredients, such as pancetta, salami, Parmesan cheese and mozzarella, are high in fat but are easily substituted with lower-fat foods, such as lean bacon and reduced-fat mozzarella, or, in many recipes, the quantity of the high-fat food can often simply be reduced to lower the fat content of the dish.

In Italy, pasta and rice dishes form a large part of the cuisine and both are ideal for a low-fat diet as they are naturally high in carbohydrates and low in fat, so long as the sauce served with the pasta or the other ingredients used for the rice dish are also low in fat!

Most of us eat fats in some form or another every day and we all need a small amount of fat in our diet to maintain a healthy, balanced eating plan. However, most of us eat far too much fat and we should all be looking to reduce our overall fat intake, especially saturated fats.

Weight for weight, dietary fats supply far more energy than all the other nutrients in our diet and if you eat a diet that is high in fat but don't exercise sufficiently to use up that energy, you will gain weight.

By cutting down on the amount of fat you eat and making easy changes to your diet, such as choosing the right types of fat, using low-fat and fat-free products whenever possible and altering the way in which you prepare and cook food, you will soon be reducing your overall fat intake and enjoying a much healthier lifestyle – and you'll hardly notice the difference!

LEFT: The abundant use of fresh vegetables and herbs in Italian cooking is ideal for a healthy low-fat eating plan.

OPPOSITE: Italian food is colourful and packed with flavour.

HEALTHY EATING GUIDELINES

A healthy diet is one that provides us with all the nutrients we need. By eating the right types, balance and proportions of foods, we are more likely to feel healthy, have plenty of energy and a higher resistance to disease that will help prevent us from developing illnesses such as heart disease, cancers, bowel disorders and obesity.

By choosing a variety of foods every day, you will ensure that you are supplying your body with all the essential nutrients, including vitamins and minerals, it needs. To get the balance right, it is important to know just how much of each type of food you should be eating.

There are five main food groups, and it is recommended that we should eat plenty of fruit and vegetables (at least five portions a day, not including potatoes) and foods such as cereals, pasta, rice and potatoes; moderate amounts of meat, fish, poultry and dairy products, and only small amounts of foods containing fat or sugar. By choosing a good balance of foods from these groups every day, and by choosing lower-fat or lower-sugar alternatives, we will be supplying our bodies with all the nutrients they need for optimum health.

THE FIVE MAIN FOOD GROUPS
- Fruit and vegetables
- Rice, potatoes, bread, pasta and other cereals
- Meat, poultry, fish and alternative proteins, such as peas, beans and lentils
- Milk and other dairy foods
- Foods that contain fat and foods that contain sugar

THE ROLE AND IMPORTANCE OF FAT IN OUR DIET

Fats shouldn't be cut out of our diets completely. We need a small amount of fat for general health and well-being – fat is a valuable source of energy, and also helps to make foods more palatable to eat. However, if you lower the fats, especially saturated fats, in your diet, it may help you to lose weight as well as reducing your risk of developing some diseases, such as heart disease.

Aim to limit your daily intake of fats to no more than 30–35 per cent of the total number of calories. Since each gram of fat provides nine calories, your total daily intake should be no more than around 70g fat. Your total intake of saturated fats should be no more than approximately ten per cent of the total number of calories.

ABOVE: By choosing a variety of foods from the five main food groups, you will ensure that you are supplying your body with all the nutrients it needs.

TYPES OF FAT

All fats in our foods are made up of building blocks of fatty acids and glycerol and their properties vary according to each combination.

There are two main types of fat, referred to as saturated and un-saturated. The unsaturated group of fats is divided into two further types – poly-unsaturated and monounsaturated fats.

There is usually a combination of these types of fat (saturated, polyunsaturated and monounsaturated) in foods that contain fat, but the amount of each type varies from one kind of food to another.

SATURATED FATS

These fats are usually hard at room temperature. They are not essential in the diet, and should be limited, as they are linked to increasing the level of cholesterol in the blood, which can increase the likelihood of heart disease.

The main sources of saturated fats are animal products, such as fatty meats, and spreading fats, such as butter and lard (shortening), that are solid at room temperature. However, there are also saturated fats of vegetable origin, notably coconut and palm oils, and some

BELOW: A selection of foods containing the three main types of fat: saturated, polyunsaturated and monounsaturated fats. Small quantities of poly- and monounsaturated fats can help to reduce the level of cholesterol in the blood.

margarines and oils, which, when processed, change the nature of the fat from unsaturated fatty acids to saturated ones. These fats are labelled "hydrogenated vegetable oil" and should be limited. Saturated fats are also found in many processed foods, such as crisps (US potato chips) and savoury snacks, as well as biscuits (cookies) and cakes.

POLYUNSATURATED FATS

There are two types of polyunsaturated fats: those of vegetable or plant origin (omega 6), such as sunflower oil, soft margarine and seeds, and those from oily fish (omega 3), such as salmon, herring, mackerel and sardines. Both fats are usually liquid at room temperature. Small quantities of polyunsaturated fats are essential for good health and are thought to help reduce the blood cholesterol level.

MONOUNSATURATED FATS

Monounsaturated fats are also thought to have the beneficial effect of reducing the blood cholesterol level and this could explain why in some Mediterranean countries there is such a low incidence of heart disease. Monounsaturated fats are found in foods such as olive oil, rapeseed (canola) oil, some nuts such as almonds and hazelnuts, oily fish and avocados.

CUTTING DOWN ON FATS AND SATURATED FATS IN THE DIET

About one-quarter of the fat we eat comes from meat and meat products, one-fifth from dairy products and margarine and the rest from cakes, biscuits, pastries and other foods.

It is relatively easy to cut down on obvious sources of fat in the diet, such as butter, oils, margarine, cream, whole milk and full-fat cheese, but we also need to know about – and check our consumption of – "hidden" fats. Hidden fats can be found in foods such as cakes, crisps, cookies and nuts.

By being aware of which foods are high in fats and particularly saturated fats, and by making simple changes to your diet, you can reduce the total fat content of your diet quite considerably.

Whenever possible, choose reduced-fat or low-fat alternatives to foods such as milk, cheese and salad dressings, and fill up on very low-fat foods, such as fruit and vegetables, and foods that are high in carbohydrates, such as pasta, rice, bread and potatoes.

Cutting down on fat doesn't mean sacrificing taste. It's easy to follow a healthy-eating plan without having to forgo all your favourite foods.

INGREDIENTS

VEGETABLES

Vegetables play an important role in Italian cooking and, as many vegetables are also naturally low in fat, they are ideal for use in low-fat Italian cooking.

AUBERGINES

Also known as eggplant, aubergines are popular in Italian cooking. Many different types can be found in Italian markets, the deep purple, elongated variety being the most common. Choose firm ones with tight, glossy skins, that feel heavy for their size.

RIGHT: Deep purple aubergines

BELOW: Clockwise from top left: beans, courgettes, potatoes, tomatoes, asparagus, carrots, peppers, broccoli and mangetout.

COURGETTES

Also called zucchini, these are widely used in Italy, both as a vegetable and for their deep yellow flowers. They are available all year round but are at their best in spring and summer. The smaller and skinnier the courgettes are, the better they taste. Choose ones that are firm with glossy green skins and avoid those which are soft or have blemished skins. Courgettes are low in calories and fat and provide some vitamin C. They are used in many low-fat Italian dishes, and are, for example, served raw in salads, cooked with other Mediterranean vegetables such as peppers and tomatoes, or simply stuffed and oven-baked.

LEFT: Courgettes

FENNEL

Fennel has become a very popular vegetable and is used widely in low-fat Italian cooking. Bulb or Florence fennel resembles a fat white celery root and has a delicate but distinctive flavour of aniseed (anise seed) and a crisp, refreshing texture. Fennel is available all year round. If possible, buy it with its feathery fronds, which you can chop and use as a herb or as a garnish. Choose fennel bulbs that feel firm with crisp white outer layers that are not wizened or yellowish. It should have a delicate, fresh scent of aniseed and the texture of green celery. Whole fennel bulbs will keep in the fridge for up to one week. Once cut, use them immediately or the cut surfaces will discolour and soften. Fennel is naturally low in calories and fat and is enjoyed in low-fat dishes throughout Italy. It is served raw in salads, lightly dressed with a vinaigrette, or sautéed, baked or braised in similar ways to celery. It is particularly good served with white fish.

RIGHT: Fennel

LEFT: Porcini mushrooms

MUSHROOMS
During the spring and autumn months, throughout the Italian countryside keen fungi collectors are spotted searching for the flavourful edible wild mushrooms that are a popular delicacy of Italy. Cultivated mushrooms, such as button (white) mushrooms, are rarely eaten in Italy, and Italians prefer to use dried or preserved wild fungi with their robust earthy taste. The most popular and highly prized mushroom used in Italian cooking is the porcini or cep, which is also readily available dried. Other popular wild mushrooms used in Italy include field (portabello) mushrooms and chanterelles.

Cultivated mushrooms and ceps can be eaten raw (in salads or lightly dressed), but other edible wild mushrooms should be cooked before eating. In Italy, mushrooms may simply be lightly grilled (broiled) or baked or added to many dishes, such as sauces, stocks, soups and risottos.

ONIONS
Onions are an essential part of Italian cooking. The varieties grown, include white, mild yellow, baby and red onions. Choose firm onions that show no signs of sprouting green leaves. Onions should have thin, almost papery skins that are unblemished. Onions are naturally low in calories and fat and they are used in numerous low-fat Italian dishes. They can be served raw in salads, stuffed and baked or, in the case of baby onions, cooked in a sweet and sour sauce of sugar and wine vinegar and served cold or hot.

PEPPERS
Generically known as capsicums, (bell) peppers come in a variety of colours including green, red, yellow, orange, white and purplish-black, all of which have a sweetish flavour and crunchy texture and can be eaten raw or cooked.

ABOVE: Mixed peppers

Each region of Italy has its own low-fat specialities using peppers. These include raw or lightly cooked peppers added to salads, roasted and lightly dressed peppers, and stuffed and oven-baked peppers.

TOMATOES
It is impossible to imagine low-fat Italian cooking without tomatoes. Tomatoes are cultivated all over Italy and are incorporated into the cooking of every region. In Italy, many types of tomatoes are grown, from plum to cherry tomatoes, and they are at their best in summer. Choose bright, firm, ripe tomatoes, with tight, unwrinkled, unblemished skins and a good aroma. Ripe tomatoes will keep well for several days in the refrigerator, but always bring tomatoes to room temperature before serving to enjoy them at their best.

Tomatoes are naturally low in calories and fat and a good source of vitamin C. They can be enjoyed raw or cooked and are often served with fresh basil leaves with which they have a great affinity. Tomatoes add flavour and colour to almost any savoury low-fat dish and can be enjoyed simply chopped and added to salads or made into a topping for bruschetta. They can be grilled, lightly fried, baked, stuffed or stewed and made into sauces and soups. Canned peeled plum tomatoes, passata (bottled strained tomatoes) and tomato purée or paste are also widely used in low-fat Italian cooking to add flavour, colour and texture to many dishes.

LEFT: Red onion

RIGHT: Vine-ripened tomatoes

FRUIT AND NUTS

The Italians prefer to enjoy fruits and nuts when they are in season and much of the fresh produce available in Italy is grown or produced locally. Most types of fruit are naturally low in fat and so play a significant part in low-fat Italian cooking to create some delicious dishes.

FIGS

Figs are grown all over Italy and there are two main types, green and purple. Both have thin, tender skins and very sweet, succulent red flesh. Choose fruits that are soft and yielding but not squashy. Fresh figs are low in calories and fat and provide some vitamin C. Fresh figs are delicious served on their own as a typical low-fat Italian dessert, but they can also be enjoyed raw or poached in both sweet and savoury low-fat dishes.

LEFT: Purple figs

ABOVE: Citrus fruits are an Italian favourite and can be used for both sweet and savoury recipes, melons make an excellent accompaniment to prosciutto as an antipasto, and cherries – usually preserved in syrup – are used in desserts.

LEMONS

Lemons are grown all over Italy and their aromatic flavour enhances many low-fat dishes. Depending on the variety, lemons may have a thick indented skin, or be perfectly smooth. Their appearance does not affect the flavour, but they should feel heavy for their size. Buy unwaxed lemons if you intend to use the zest in recipes. Lemons will keep in the refrigerator for up to two weeks. They are low in calories and fat and provide a good source of vitamin C. Lemons are very versatile and the juice and/or zest is added to many low-fat Italian dishes. Lemon is used in cold drinks, to add flavour to dressings and sauces, freshly squeezed over

cooked fish or lean meat to add flavour, or as an aromatic flavouring for low-fat cakes and baked goods.

MELONS

Many different varieties of sweet aromatic melons are grown in Italy, the most common types being cantaloupe melons and watermelons. The best way to tell whether a melon is ripe is to smell it; it should have a mild, sweet scent. If it smells highly perfumed and musky it will be over-ripe. The fruit should feel heavy for its size and the skin should not be bruised or damaged. Gently press the rind with your thumbs at the stalk end; it should give a little. Melons are low in calories and fat and a source of vitamin C. Typically, Italians enjoy melon as an appetizer, simply served on its own or with wafer-thin slices of prosciutto, or as a tasty dessert on its own, in a fresh fruit salad, or as a sorbet (sherbert) or granita.

BELOW: Watermelon

ABOVE: The Italian climate is perfect for growing oranges; they add a bright splash of colour to salads and desserts.

ORANGES

Many varieties of oranges are grown in Sicily and southern Italy, the best-known Sicilian oranges being the small blood oranges with their bright ruby-red flesh. Other types include sweet navel and bitter oranges. Choose unwaxed oranges if you intend to use the zest in recipes. Oranges are naturally low in calories and fat and provide a good source of vitamin C. Oranges are served in both sweet and savoury low-fat dishes across Italy, including in salads, desserts, sorbets or granitas.

PEACHES AND NECTARINES

Peaches and nectarines with their sweet juicy flesh are summer fruits grown in Italy. Both fruits are available in either yellow or

ABOVE: Peaches

white fleshed varieties, all of which are succulent, juicy and full of flavour. They are naturally low in calories and fat and provide some vitamin C. Peaches and nectarines are interchangeable in recipes and are delicious served as a dessert fruit but can also be macerated in fortified wine or spirits or poached in white wine or syrup to create a typical low-fat Italian dessert. They are also delicious served with raspberries or made into fruit drinks, low-fat ice creams and sorbets.

ALMONDS AND OTHER NUTS

Two varieties of almonds are grown in Italy – sweet and bitter almonds. Sweet almonds are the most common and are eaten on their own or used in cooking and baking. Bitter almonds (illegal in the US), are not edible raw and are used to flavour liqueurs such as amaretto. In Italy, sweet almonds are enjoyed raw as a dessert or dried and blanched, slivered or ground for use in cakes and baked goods. Dried sweet almonds are the most common type used in many countries. Almonds are high in monounsaturated fat and low in saturated fat.

Other nuts, such as hazelnuts, walnuts and pistachios, are also grown and harvested in Italy and are used in many sweet and savoury dishes, including desserts, confectionary, cakes and baked goods. Hazelnuts are usually dried before use, whereas walnuts can be enjoyed fresh or dried and pistachios are eaten raw or roasted. As with many nuts, they are all high in fat, although the type of fats they contain are the "healthier" types

LEFT: Pine nuts (top) and almonds (below)

– either monounsaturated or poly-unsaturated fats. They are all low in saturated fat but should be used sparingly in low-fat cooking.

PINE NUTS

Pine nuts or pine kernels are very popular in Italy and are an essential ingredient in the classic Italian pesto sauce. They can be eaten either raw or toasted and are used in both sweet and savoury dishes. Pine nuts are high in polyunsaturated fat and low in saturated fat and they should be used in moderation.

BELOW: Almonds are an extremely versatile ingredient, used raw or to flavour cakes and liqueurs. Red and white Italian grapes are particularly refreshing on a hot day; they have a wonderful Muscat flavour.

PASTA

Pasta is the one ingredient that probably sums up the essence of Italian cooking, and it is an essential part of many Italian meals. It is a wonderfully simple, nutritious and low-fat food which is available in a whole wealth of shapes and sizes. There are two basic types of pasta: dried and fresh.

FRESH PASTA

Home-made fresh pasta is usually made by hand using superfine plain white flour enriched with eggs. It is often wrapped around a low-fat stuffing of lean meat, fish, vegetables or low-fat cheese to make filled pasta such as ravioli or tortellini, or layered with lean meat or vegetable sauces to make a tasty low-fat lasagne. Commercially-made fresh pasta is made with durum wheat, water and eggs. The flavour and texture of all fresh pasta is very delicate, so it is best suited to slightly more creamy, low-fat sauces.

DRIED PASTA

Dried pasta is produced from a dough made from hard durum wheat. It is then shaped into different forms, from long, thin spaghetti to elaborate spirals and frilly bow shapes. Dried pasta can be made from basic pasta dough, which consists of durum wheat and water, or it can be made from a dough enriched with eggs or coloured and flavoured with ingredients such as

LEFT: Dried rigatoni

ABOVE: Fresh pasta comes in a wide variety of interesting shapes, sizes and colours.

LEFT: Capelli d'angelo

RIGHT: Fettucine

spinach, herbs, tomatoes or squid ink. Dried pasta has a nutty flavour and should always retain a firm texture when cooked. It is generally used in preference to fresh pasta for thinner-textured, more robust, low-fat sauces.

BUYING AND STORING PASTA

Choose dried pasta that is made from Italian durum wheat and store it in a cool, dry place. Once opened, dried pasta will keep for weeks in an airtight container. Home-made fresh pasta will only keep for a couple of days, but it also freezes very well. Commercially made fresh pasta (fresh pasta that is available in a chilled compartment in the supermarket) is

RIGHT: Dried spaghetti

pasteurized and vacuum-packed, so it will keep in the refrigerator for about two weeks, or it can be frozen for up to six months. When buying coloured and flavoured pasta, make sure that it has been made with natural ingredients.

COOKING PASTA

All pasta must be cooked in a large pan filled with plenty of fast-boiling, salted water. Cooking times vary according to the type, size and shape of the pasta but, as a general rule, filled pasta takes about 12 minutes, dried pasta needs 8–10 minutes and fresh pasta only 2–3 minutes. All pasta should be cooked until it is *al dente*, or still firm to the bite. Always test pasta for readiness just before you think it should be done as it can easily overcook. To stop it cooking, take the pan off the heat and run a little cold water into it, then drain the pasta and serve.

PASTA VARIETIES

Pasta shapes can be divided roughly into four categories: long strands or ribbons, flat, short and filled. When choosing the appropriate pasta for a sauce, there are no hard-and-fast rules; almost any pasta is suitable for a low-fat sauce.

LEFT: Conchiglie

BELOW: Tomato and spinach orecchiette

SHORT PASTA

Short pasta covers a wide variety of shapes, the more common types being macaroni, rigati, rigatoni and tubetti. Pasta shapes vary and the list is almost endless, with some wonderfully descriptive names. There are cappellacci (little hats), orecchiette (little ears) or maltagliati (badly cut) and penne (quills), conchiglie (little shells), farfalle (bows) and lumache (snails).

LONG OR RIBBON PASTA

The best-known long variety is spaghetti, which also comes in a thinner version, spaghettini, and the flatter linguine, which means "little tongues". Bucatini are thicker and hollow – perfect for trapping low-fat sauces in the cavity. Ribbon pasta is wider than the strands and fettucine, tagliatelle and trenette all fall into this category. Dried tagliatelle is usually sold folded into nests, which unravel during cooking. Pappardelle are the widest ribbon pasta; they are often served with a low-fat rabbit sauce. The thinnest pasta strands are vermicelli (little worms) and ultra-fine capelli d'angelo (angel's hair).

FLAT PASTA

In Italy, fresh flat pasta is often called maccheroni, not to be confused with the short tubes of macaroni with which we are familiar. Lasagne and cannelloni are larger flat rectangles of pasta, used for layering or rolling round a low-fat filling; dried cannelloni are already formed into wide tubes. Layered pasta dishes like this are cooked in the oven.

RIGHT: Lasagne

BELOW: Multi-coloured tagliatelle

RIGHT: Tortelli

FILLED PASTA

Dried and fresh filled pastas are available in many varieties and there are dozens of names for filled pasta, but the only difference lies in the shape and size. Ravioli are square, tortelli and agnolotti are usually round, while tortellini and anellini are ring-shaped. Fillings for fresh and dried pasta include lean meat, pumpkin, artichokes, ricotta and spinach, shellfish, chicken and mushrooms.

GNOCCHI

Gnocchi fall into a different category from other pasta, being similar to small dumplings. They can be made from semolina (milled durum wheat), flour, potatoes or ricotta and spinach and may be shaped like elongated shells, ovals, cylinders or flat discs, or roughly shredded into strozzapreti (priest stranglers). Gnocchi are extremely light and almost melt in the mouth and can be served like any pasta, as a low-fat first course, in clear soup or as an accompaniment to the main course.

RIGHT: Gnocchi

BREAD, RICE, GRAINS AND BEANS

ABOVE: Ciabatta

Rice, grains and beans form the basis of many delicious and nutritious low-fat Italian dishes and fresh bread is always served in Italy as a tasty, low-fat accompaniment to every meal.

In Italy, no meal is ever served without bread. There are numerous different types of Italian breads with many regional variations. Several varieties, such as ciabatta and focaccia are readily available from bakers or supermarkets.

Rice and grains are staple foods in Italy and are almost as important as pasta in Italian cooking. Italy relied heavily on these low-fat, protein-rich foods when luxuries such as meat were in short supply, and a whole host of wholesome and delicious low-fat recipes were developed using these modest ingredients.

Many beans, both fresh and dried, are naturally low in fat and are used widely in low-fat Italian cooking, providing the basis for a variety of delicious dishes.

CIABATTA

These flattish, slipper-shaped loaves with squared or rounded ends are made with olive oil and are often flavoured with fresh or dried herbs, olives or sun-dried tomatoes. They have an airy texture inside and a pale, crisp crust. Ciabatta is delicious served warm and is excellent for low-fat sandwiches.

FOCACCIA

Focaccia is a dimpled flat bread similar to pizza dough which is traditionally lightly oiled and baked in a wood oven. A whole traditional focaccia from an Italian bakery weighs several pounds (kilos) and is sold by weight, cut into manageable pieces. A variety of low-fat ingredients can be worked into the dough or served as a topping – onions, rosemary or oregano, lean ham or olives.

LEFT: Focaccia

RIGHT: Risotto rices like these arborio varieties are famous in Italy, and can be flavoured with an almost endless array of ingredients.

RICE

Italy produces a great variety of rice including the short-grain carnaroli and arborio rice, which make the best risottos. Italian rice is classified by size, ranging from the shortest, roundest ordinario (used for puddings), to semifino (for soups and salads), then fino and finally the longer grains of the finest risotto rice, superfino.

Rice is used in many low-fat Italian dishes. Baked rice dishes are also popular or plain boiled rice may simply be served on its own.

The most famous of all Italian rice dishes, however, is risotto. A good risotto can be made only with superfine rice and provides a delicious low-fat Italian meal. All risottos are basically prepared in the same way, although they can be flavoured with an almost endless variety of exciting ingredients.

Buy only superfine risotto rice for use in Italian risottos. Shorter grain rice is best reserved for making soups and puddings. Store uncooked rice in an airtight container in a cool, dry place. The rice will keep for several months.

ABOVE: Fine polenta

POLENTA

For centuries, polenta has been a staple low-fat food of northern Italy. It is a grainy yellow flour which is a type of corn meal made from ground maize. It is then cooked into a kind of porridge and used in a variety of ways. There are two main types of polenta – coarse and fine.

Polenta is very versatile and can be used to create many delicious low-fat dishes. It is most often served in Italy as a first

LEFT: Dried cannellini beans

ABOVE: Canned borlotti beans

LEFT: Canned black-eyed beans

course but it can also be used as a vegetable dish or main course. Plain boiled polenta can be served on its own to make a satisfying dish. It goes well with lean meats and game or it can be cooled and cut into squares before being grilled (broiled) or baked and served with a low-fat sauce or topping.

Quick-cooking polenta, which can be prepared in only five minutes, and ready-prepared blocks of cooked polenta are also available, but traditional polenta only takes about 20 minutes to cook, so it is best to buy this for its superior texture and flavour. Once opened, polenta will keep in an airtight container for at least one month.

HARICOT BEANS

Haricot (navy) beans are eaten all over Italy, the most popular varieties being borlotti beans, cannellini beans (a type of kidney bean) and black-eyed beans. All these are eaten in hearty low-fat stews, with pasta, in low-fat soups or salads or simply cooked and served as a side dish.

Both fresh and dried beans are available in Italy and canned varieties make an acceptable substitute. Once opened, store dried beans in an airtight container in a cool, dry place for up to one year.

BROAD BEANS

Broad (fava) beans are at their best when eaten fresh from the pod in late spring or early summer when they are small and very tender, or cooked and skinned later in the season. They are popular in Italy and are excellent served with lean ham,

LEFT: Canned broad beans

in other low-fat dishes such as risotto or simply served as a vegetable accompaniment. Dried broad beans, which need pre-cooking, are also used in Italian dishes such as low-fat soups and stews.

CHICKPEAS

Chickpeas, which are round, golden and shaped rather like hazelnuts, and which have a distinctive, nutty flavour, are also popular in low-fat Italian cooking. Chickpeas are cooked and used in the same way as haricot beans and they can also be served cold and lightly dressed to make a tasty salad.

LENTILS

Lentils grow in pods although they are always sold podded and dried. Italian lentils are the small brown variety which do not break up during cooking and are often mixed with pasta or rice to create delicious and satisfying low-fat dishes. They are also delicious served cold, lightly dressed or in nutritious soups. Whole brown, green or puy lentils can also be used.

ABOVE: Dried chickpeas

RIGHT: Dried brown lentils

MEAT, POULTRY AND FISH

Although meat and poultry did not feature largely in Italian cooking until more recent years, a variety of lean cuts and a range of fish are used in many appetizing low-fat Italian dishes.

LEFT: Prosciutto di Parma

RIGHT: Lamb cutlets

CURED MEATS

Italy is famous for its prosciutto crudo – salted and dried ham that requires no cooking. The most famous of these hams is prosciutto di Parma, or Parma ham, which has a medium fat content, but is served in wafer-thin slices, so can be incorporated into low-fat Italian dishes.

Pancetta, bresaola, mortadella and salami are also popular Italian cured meats. Meats such as pancetta, mortadella and salami are high in fat and should be used sparingly in low-fat Italian recipes. Bresaola has a similar fat content to prosciutto or Parma ham.

BELOW: Bresaola

BEEF

Lean, thick T-bone steaks are a popular choice in Italy and are often simply cooked over wood fires. Beef olives are also popular and leftover cooked lean beef can be sliced and made into a tasty salad. Less tender cuts of beef are usually braised, stewed or minced (ground) and used for a whole variety of tasty low-fat Italian dishes. Choose lean cuts of beef which are naturally low in fat or choose extra-lean minced beef.

ABOVE: Minced beef

CHICKEN AND TURKEY

Poultry is a popular food in Italy and is used to create a huge variety of simple and delicious, low-fat Italian dishes. Factory farming does exist in Italy but many flavoursome free-range birds are also available. Chicken and turkey are usually filleted for quick cooking, and removing and discarding the skin before cooking ensures the meat is very lean.

LAMB

Lambs in Italy are bred mainly in the southern region and they are slaughtered at different ages, resulting in distinctive flavours. Young spring lambs are often spit-roasted whole or used for roasting or grilling. Older lamb has a stronger flavour and is suitable for roasting or stewing. Choose lean cuts of lamb for low-fat cooking to keep the fat content down.

PORK

A lot of Italian pork is transformed into hams, sausages and salamis, but fresh pork is also enjoyed all over Italy. Lean

BELOW: Chicken

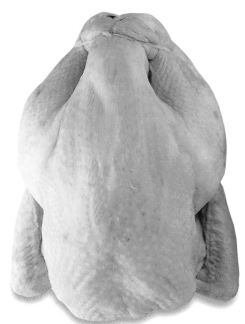

ABOVE: Rabbit

pork chops can be grilled (broiled) or braised with herbs or artichokes for a tasty, low-fat meal. Loin of pork can be braised in milk or roasted with rosemary or sage. Choose lean cuts of pork and remove and discard any visible fat before cooking to keep the fat content low.

RABBIT

Rabbit often replaces chicken or veal in low-fat Italian cooking. The meat is very pale and is naturally lean and low in fat. Wild rabbit has a stronger flavour; farmed rabbit is very tender and has a much more delicate flavour. Farmed rabbit can replace chicken or turkey in almost any low-fat recipe. Wild rabbit can be stewed or braised in white wine or Marsala, or with aubergines (eggplant), lean bacon and tomatoes. It can also be roasted simply with root vegetables or fresh herbs.

FISH

Italy's extensive coastal waters are host to a large variety of fish and shellfish, many of which are unknown outside Italy. Italians like their fish very fresh and tend to cook it simply. Large fish are usually

grilled, cooked on a barbecue or baked; smaller whole fish may be stuffed and grilled or baked, and small fry are often lightly pan-fried.

Popular fish in Italy include white fish such as monkfish, cod and sole and oily fish such as salmon, swordfish, tuna, trout or sardines. Some fish are dried, salted or preserved in oil, the most popular being tuna which is packed in olive oil. Salted dried cod is also a favourite which is often made into soups and stews.

White fish is very low in fat and is ideal for use in low-fat Italian cooking. Remove and discard the skin to keep the fat content low. Oily fish such as tuna and swordfish are also naturally low in fat and although oily fish such as salmon is higher in fat, it is higher in the "healthier" types of fat – poly-unsaturated and monounsaturated fats – and low in saturated fat.

BELOW: Prawns

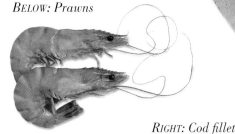

RIGHT: Cod fillet

SHELLFISH

The Italians enjoy a huge variety of shellfish and crustaceans from their coastal waters and almost all shellfish are considered edible, from mussels, clams and scallops to octopus, squid, razor-shells and sea snails. Shrimps and prawns come in all sizes and colours, from

ABOVE: Fish and shellfish, such as sardines and mussels, are often simply grilled or fried, or used as the basis of a soup or stew.

vibrant red to pale grey, while crustaceans range from bright orange crawfish to blue-black lobsters.

Most shellfish and crustaceans are nutritious, naturally low in fat and ideal for creating many delicious low-fat Italian dishes. Squid and cuttlefish are served cut into rings either as part of a shellfish salad or before being lightly fried with other types of fish. Octopus tend to be cooked slowly for long periods to tenderize them or, if very small ones are available, these can be cooked in the same way as squid.

Mussels make an attractive and tasty addition to many low-fat pasta and fish dishes, salads and pizza toppings. They are especially good served with a low-fat garlic tomato sauce. Shrimps and prawns can be boiled and served with lemon juice and olive oil or in salads. They can also be grilled and served with tomato sauce or rice.

DAIRY PRODUCTS

Dairy products such as butter and cheeses play a part in low-fat Italian cooking but due to their generally high fat content they should only be used in small amounts.

LEFT: Butter

RIGHT: Mozzarella

BUTTER

Although olive oil is the primary fat used for cooking in Italy, butter is used more commonly in northern Italian cooking. The quantity of butter used in recipes in this book has been kept to a minimum as butter is very high in fat, particularly saturated fat. Choose a polyunsaturated or mono-unsaturated margarine in place of butter if you prefer. Although the fat content of these margarines is similar to butter, the fats are "healthier" types. Very low-fat spreads are not suitable for cooking; only use these for spreading.

CHEESES

Italy has a great variety of cheese, ranging from fresh, mild cheese such as mozzarella to mature (sharp) hard cheeses such as Parmesan. All types of milk are used, including cow's, ewe's, goat's and buffalo's and some cheeses are made from a mixture of milks. Other popular types of Italian cheese include Pecorino, Provolone, Bel Paese, Fontina, ricotta, Gorgonzola and mascarpone.

Many of the Italian cheeses are suitable for cooking and are used in a wide variety of dishes. However, many are also high in fat, especially saturated fat, but if used in moderation can be incorporated into low-fat Italian cuisine. Strong-flavoured cheeses, such as Parmesan, can be used in smaller quantities and other cheeses, such as mozzarella, are available in reduced-fat versions.

ABOVE: Parmesan

PARMESAN

Parmesan is the best-known and most important of the Italian hard cheeses. There are two basic types – Parmigiano Reggiano and Grana Padano – but the former is infinitely superior. A little finely grated Parmesan adds delicious flavour to many dishes from pasta and polenta to risotto and minestrone.

LEFT: Pecorino studded with peppercorns

RIGHT: Ricotta

MOZZARELLA

Italian cooking could hardly exist without mozzarella, the pure white egg-shaped fresh cheese, whose melting quality makes it perfect for so many dishes. The best mozzarella is made in the area around Naples, using water buffalo's milk. Reduced-fat mozzarella is also readily available and is ideal for use in low-fat Italian cooking. It is delicious in sandwiches or served with fresh red tomatoes and green basil (*insalata tricolore*, or three-colour salad). When cooked, mozzarella becomes uniquely stringy and is ideal for topping pizzas.

RICOTTA

Ricotta is a fresh, soft cheese made from cow's, ewe's or goat's milk. It is used widely in Italy for both sweet and savoury recipes. Ricotta has a medium fat content so should be used in moderation in low-fat Italian cooking. It has an excellent texture and a mild flavour, so it makes a perfect vehicle for seasonings such as black pepper, nutmeg or chopped fresh herbs. It is also puréed with cooked spinach to make a classic filling for ravioli, cannelloni or lasagne. It is often used in desserts and it can be sweetened and then served with fresh fruit.

OLIVE OIL AND FLAVOURINGS

Olive oil and flavourings play an important role in Italian cooking. They are ideal for combining with staples such as rice and pasta to create speedy and nutritious low-fat meals.

OLIVE OIL

Olive oil is perhaps the single most important ingredient in an Italian kitchen. The best olive oil is extra virgin, which must have an acidity level of less than one per cent. It is ideal for using "raw" in salad dressings, uncooked sauces and for drizzling lightly over vegetables. Virgin olive oil has a higher acidity level and less refined flavour and is used as a condiment or for general cooking. Unclassified or pure olive oil is refined, then blended with virgin oil to add flavour and is ideal for cooking and baking.

Olive oil is high in monounsaturated fat and low in saturated fat and should be used in moderation when preparing low-fat Italian recipes.

LEFT: Extra virgin olive oil

BELOW: Balsamic vinegar

ABOVE: A selection of flavourings essential for the authentic Italian pantry. Here we see a variety of oils, sun-dried tomatoes and tomato paste, passata, anchovies, capers and balsamic vinegar.

RIGHT: A mixture of black and green olives

BALSAMIC VINEGAR

Balsamic vinegar is the king of vinegars and is made in the area around Modena in Italy. It is the boiled and concentrated juice of local trebbiano grapes, which is aged over a very long period to give it a slightly syrupy texture and a rich, deep mahogany colour. Balsamic vinegar is used as a dressing or to finish a delicate sauce for white fish, poultry or calf's liver.

OLIVES

Black and green olives are used in low-fat Italian cooking, and both types are available whole or pitted, sold loose, in jars or vacuum-packed. Olives are added to many low-fat Italian dishes, such as salads and sauces. Olives are quite high in monounsaturated fat and low in saturated fat, but should be used in moderation.

PESTO

Green pesto is traditionally made with fresh basil, pine nuts, Parmesan and olive oil, but a red version based on sweet red (bell) peppers is also available. It can be home-made or bought ready-made in jars or fresh in tubs. Pesto can be added to hot pasta, gnocchi, risottos and tomato-based sauces and soups. However, pesto is high in fat and should be used sparingly.

SUN-DRIED TOMATOES

Wrinkled red sun-dried tomatoes are available dry in packets or preserved in oil in jars. Dry-packed tomatoes are lower in fat than the oil-packed ones and are used in many low-fat Italian dishes to add flavour and colour. They can be eaten on their own as a snack, or soaked in hot water until soft, then added to numerous dishes including low-fat sauces, soups, egg and vegetable dishes.

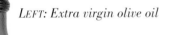

RIGHT: Sun-dried tomatoes

HERBS AND SPICES

Herbs and spices are vital to low-fat Italian cooking. Their aromatic flavour adds depth and interest to numerous dishes. Many wild herbs grow in the Italian countryside and are often incorporated into low-fat Italian recipes. Buy growing herbs in their pots if you can as this ensures the herbs are as fresh as possible. Better still, grow herbs in your own kitchen garden, in tubs or on windowsills and enjoy the convenience of a continuous supply.

ABOVE: Always use fresh herbs whenever you can. Their aromatic flavour adds depth and interest to all Italian cooking.

LEFT: Basil

RIGHT: Rosemary

BASIL

Basil, with its intense aroma and fresh, pungently sweet flavour, is associated with low-fat Italian cooking more than any other herb. There are many varieties of fresh basil but sweet basil is the most common. It is an essential ingredient of pesto, but it is also used in low-fat soups, salads, white fish and shellfish dishes and almost any dish based on tomatoes, with which it has a great affinity. It is best added at the end of cooking.

MARJORAM AND OREGANO

These two highly aromatic herbs are closely related (oregano is the wild variety), but marjoram has a much milder flavour. Marjoram is more

ABOVE: Marjoram

RIGHT: Parsley

commonly used in northern Italy, to flavour meat, poultry, vegetables and low-fat soups, while oregano is widely used in the south to flavour low-fat tomato dishes, vegetables and pizza. Choose plants which have fresh-looking leaves of good colour and even size.

PARSLEY

Italian parsley is the flat leaf variety which has a more robust flavour than curly parsley. It is used in low-fat savoury dishes such as soups, sauces, stocks, stews and risottos. Chopped parsley or whole leaves may also be used as a garnish. If flat leaf parsley is not available, curly parsley makes a good substitute. Choose parsley which has a good, fresh green colour.

ROSEMARY

Spiky evergreen rosemary bushes, with their attractive blue flowers, grow wild all over Italy. The herb has a delicious, highly aromatic flavour which can easily overpower a dish, so should be used sparingly. Rosemary combines well with roast or grilled lean lamb, veal and chicken. It is also used to enhance low-fat dishes such as those based on baked fish and tomato. Some rosemary branches added to the charcoal on a barbecue impart a lovely flavour to whatever is being cooked.

SAGE

Wild sage grows in profusion in the Italian countryside. There are several varieties, all of which have a slightly bitter, aromatic flavour, which contrasts well with lean meat such as pork, veal and chicken. Sage should be used sparingly and combines well with almost all low-fat meat and vegetable dishes, including minestrone, calf's liver and white haricot (navy) beans. Choose leaves that look fresh and bright in colour. Fresh sage should be stored in a plastic bag in the refrigerator for up to one week.

RIGHT: Sage

BELOW: Black peppercorns

BLACK PEPPERCORNS

Black peppercorns are the green berries of a vine, which are dried on mats in the sun until they are all wrinkled and black. They are used for seasoning numerous low-fat Italian dishes and are best used freshly ground in a mill or crushed to enjoy their delicious flavour and aroma. Store peppercorns in an airtight container in a cool, dry place.

CHILLIES

Chopped fresh chillies or hot flakes of dried chillies are added to many low-fat Italian dishes. Fresh chillies vary in taste, from mild to fiery hot and they are unusual in that their "hotness" is usually in inverse proportion to their size, so larger, round fleshly varieties are generally milder than the smaller, thin-skinned pointed ones. For a milder spicy flavour, remove and discard the seeds and veins from fresh chillies before use. A small pinch of dried chilli flakes spices up low-fat stews and sauces, particularly those made with tomatoes. For a really hot low-fat pizza,

RIGHT: Fresh red chillies

crumble a few dried chilli flakes over the top. Dried chillies are extremely fiery and should be used sparingly.

Take care when preparing fresh chillies and always wear rubber or plastic gloves, or wash your hands and utensils thoroughly after use as chillies contain volatile oils which can irritate and burn if they touch sensitive areas, especially the eyes.

SAFFRON

Saffron is the world's most expensive spice and consists of the hand-picked dried stigmas of the saffron crocus. It has a highly aromatic flavour and will impart a rich golden colour to many dishes. In Italy, saffron is mainly used to flavour and colour risottos and it is excellent in low-fat sauces for fish and poultry. It can also be used to flavour biscuits (cookies) and cakes. Saffron threads are sold in small boxes or jars containing only a few grams, and powdered saffron is also available in jars.

SALT

Salt is the universal seasoning ingredient used to bring out the flavour of both sweet and savoury dishes. It is odourless but strongly flavoured and without it our food would be insipid and bland. Several types of salt are widely available, including rock salt, sea salt and refined

ABOVE: Saffron threads

table salt. Due to its strong flavour, salt should be used sparingly in cooking and for seasoning food. Always store salt in an airtight container in a cool, dry place.

LEFT: Fine and coarse sea salt

BELOW: Italian chillies are generally milder than their South American counterparts, but should still be used with caution – it can often be quite difficult to gauge their heat.

THE FAT AND CALORIE CONTENTS OF FOOD

The following figures show the weight of fat (g) and the energy content per 100g/3½oz of each food.

VEGETABLES	FAT (G)	ENERGY
Aubergines (eggplant), raw	0.4	15Kcals/64kJ
Aubergines, fried in corn oil	31.9	302Kcals/1262kJ
Artichokes, globe, raw	0.2	18Kcals/77kJ
Broccoli, raw	0.9	33Kcals/138kJ
Carrots, raw	0.3	35Kcals/146kJ
Cauliflowers, raw	0.9	34Kcals/142kJ
Chard, Swiss, raw	0.2	19Kcals/81kJ
Chicory (Belgian endive), raw	0.6	11Kcals/45kJ
Courgettes (zucchini), raw	0.4	18Kcals/74kJ
Cucumbers, raw	0.1	10Kcals/40kJ
Fennel, Florence, raw	0.2	12Kcals/50kJ
Mushrooms, raw	0.4	13Kcals/55kJ
Olives, in brine	11.0	103Kcals/422kJ
Onions, raw	0.2	36Kcals/150kJ
Peas, raw	1.5	83Kcals/344kJ
(Bell) Peppers, red, raw	0.4	32Kcals/134kJ
Potatoes, raw	0.2	75Kcals/318kJ
Radicchio, raw	0.2	14Kcals/58kJ
Spinach, raw	0.8	25Kcals/103kJ
Squash, butternut	0.1	36Kcals/155kJ
Tomatoes, raw	0.3	17Kcals/73kJ

FRUIT AND NUTS	FAT (G)	ENERGY
Apples, eating, raw	0.1	47Kcals/199kJ
Apricots, raw	0.1	31Kcals/134kJ
Avocados	19.5	190Kcals/748kJ
Bananas	0.3	95Kcals/403kJ
Dried mixed fruit	0.4	268Kcals/1144kJ
Figs, raw	0.3	43Kcals/185kJ
Figs, ready-to-eat (dried)	1.5	209Kcals/889kJ
Grapefruits, raw	0.1	30Kcals/126kJ
Grapes	0.1	60Kcals/257kJ
Melons	0.1	24Kcals/102kJ
Nectarines	0.1	40Kcals/171kJ
Oranges	0.1	37Kcals/158kJ
Peaches	0.1	33Kcals/142kJ
Pears	0.1	40Kcals/169kJ
Almonds	55.8	612Kcals/2534kJ
Brazil nuts	68.2	682Kcals/2813kJ
Cashew nuts, plain	48.2	573Kcals/2374kJ
Chestnuts	2.7	170Kcals/719kJ
Hazelnuts	63.5	650Kcals/2685kJ
Pine nuts	68.6	688Kcals/2840kJ
Pistachio nuts	55.4	601Kcals/2485kJ
Walnuts	68.5	688Kcals/2837kJ

CEREALS AND BAKING	FAT (G)	ENERGY
Brown rice, uncooked	2.8	357Kcals/1518kJ
White rice, uncooked	3.6	383Kcals/1630kJ
Pasta, white, uncooked	1.8	342Kcals/1456kJ
Pasta, wholewheat, uncooked	2.5	324Kcals/1379kJ
Brown bread	2.0	218Kcals/927kJ
White bread	1.9	235Kcals/1002kJ
Wholemeal (whole-wheat) bread	2.5	215Kcals/914kJ
Sugar, white	0	394Kcals/1680kJ
Chocolate, milk	30.7	520Kcals/2177kJ
Chocolate, plain (semisweet)	28.0	510Kcals/2137kJ
Honey	0	288Kcals/1229kJ
Fruit jam	0	261Kcals/1114kJ

BEANS	FAT (G)	ENERGY
Black-eyed beans (peas), cooked	0.7	116Kcals/494kJ
Broad (fava) beans, raw	1.0	59Kcals/247kJ
Butter (lima) beans, canned	0.5	77Kcals/327kJ
Chickpeas, canned	2.9	115Kcals/487kJ
Green and brown lentils, cooked	0.7	105Kcals/446kJ
Red kidney beans, canned	0.6	100Kcals/424kJ

MEAT AND MEAT PRODUCTS	FAT (G)	ENERGY	DAIRY, FATS AND OILS	FAT (G)	ENERGY
Bacon, streaky (fatty), raw	23.6	276Kcals/1142kJ	Cream, double (heavy)	48.0	449Kcals/1849kJ
Bacon, lean back, raw	6.7	136Kcals/568kJ	Cream, single (light)	19.1	198Kcals/817kJ
Beef, minced (ground), raw	16.2	225Kcals/934kJ	Crème fraîche	40.0	379Kcals/156kJ
Beef, minced, extra lean, raw	9.6	174Kcals/728kJ	Reduced-fat crème fraîche	15.0	165Kcals/683kJ
Beef, average, lean, raw	5.1	136Kcals/571kJ	Reduced-fat double cream	24.0	243Kcals/1002kJ
Lamb, average, lean, raw	8.3	156Kcals/651kJ	Milk, skimmed	0.1	33Kcals/140kJ
Pork, average, lean, raw	4.0	123Kcals/519kJ	Milk, whole	3.9	66Kcals/275kJ
Chicken breast, no skin, raw	1.1	106Kcals/449kJ	Cheddar cheese	34.4	412Kcals/1708kJ
Chicken, roasted, meat and skin	12.5	218Kcals/910kJ	Cheddar-type, reduced-fat	15.0	261Kcals/1091kJ
Duck, meat only, raw	6.5	137Kcals/575kJ	Cream cheese	47.4	439Kcals/1807kJ
Duck, roasted, meat, fat, skin	38.1	423Kcals/1750kJ	Fromage frais, plain	7.1	113Kcals/469kJ
Turkey, meat only, raw	1.6	105Kcals/443kJ	Fromage frais, very low-fat	0.2	58Kcals/247kJ
Liver, lamb, raw	6.2	137Kcals/575kJ	Mozzarella cheese	21.0	289Kcals/1204kJ
Salami	39.2	438Kcals/1814kJ	Ricotta cheese	11.0	144Kcals/599kJ
Prosciutto	12.7	223Kcals/932kJ	Skimmed milk soft cheese	Trace	74Kcals/313kJ
Liver, calf, raw	3.4	104Kcals/437kJ	Feta cheese	20.2	250Kcals/1037kJ
			Parmesan cheese	32.7	452Kcals/1880kJ

FISH AND SHELLFISH	FAT (G)	ENERGY			
Anchovies, canned in oil	19.9	280Kcals/1165kJ	Low-fat yogurt, natural (plain)	0.8	56Kcals/236kJ
Clams, canned in brine	0.6	77Kcals/325kJ	Greek (US strained plain) yogurt	9.1	115Kcals/477kJ
Cod fillets, raw	0.7	80Kcals/337kJ	Reduced-fat Greek yogurt	5.0	80Kcals/335kJ
Crab, canned	0.5	77Kcals/326kJ	Butter	81.7	737Kcals/3031kJ
Haddock, raw	0.6	81Kcals/345kJ	Margarine	81.6	739Kcals/3039kJ
Monkfish, raw	0.4	66Kcals/282kJ	Low-fat spread	40.5	39Kcals/1605kJ
Mussels, raw	1.8	74Kcals/312kJ	Very low-fat spread	25.0	273Kcals/1128kJ
Plaice or flounder, raw	1.4	79Kcals/336kJ	Corn oil	99.9	899Kcals/3696kJ
Prawns (shrimp), boiled	0.9	99Kcals/418kJ	Olive oil	99.9	899Kcals/3696kJ
Red mullet (snapper), raw	3.8	109Kcals/459kJ	Safflower oil	99.9	899Kcals/3696kJ
Sardines, raw	9.2	165Kcals/691kJ	Eggs, whole, raw	10.8	147Kcals/612kJ
Sea bass, raw	2.5	100Kcals/421kJ	Egg yolk, raw	30.5	339Kcals/1402kJ
Squid, raw	1.7	81Kcals/344kJ	Egg white, raw	Trace	36Kcals/153kJ
Tuna, canned in brine	0.6	99Kcals/422kJ	Dressing, fat-free	1.2	67Kcals/282kJ
Tuna, canned in oil	9.0	189Kcals/794kJ	Dressing, French	49.4	462Kcals/1902kJ
Tuna, raw	4.6	136Kcals/573kJ	Mayonnaise	75.6	691Kcals/2843kJ
			Mayonnaise, reduced-calorie	28.1	288Kcals/1188kJ

SOUPS, SALADS AND APPETIZERS

HEALTHY *and* REFRESHING *salads and appetizers can provide a* TEMPTING *start to a meal.* DELICIOUS *soups can be made in no time and make for an ideal first course, or a complete* LIGHT *meal on their own. Choose and enjoy from dishes such as* WILD *Mushroom Soup,* ROASTED *Plum Tomatoes with Garlic, and Melon, Prosciutto and* STRAWBERRY *Salad.*

TOMATO AND FRESH BASIL SOUP

A soup for late summer, when fresh plum tomatoes are at their most flavoursome, this fresh tomato soup flavoured with basil creates a tasty supper dish.

2 Stir in the chopped tomatoes and garlic, then add the stock, white wine and tomato paste, with salt and pepper to taste. Bring to the boil, then reduce the heat, half-cover the pan and simmer gently for 20 minutes, stirring the mixture occasionally to stop the tomatoes from sticking to the base of the pan.

3 Purée the soup with the shredded basil in a blender or food processor until smooth, then press through a sieve into a clean pan. Discard the remaining contents of the sieve.

INGREDIENTS
15ml/1 tbsp olive oil
1 onion, finely chopped
900g/2lb ripe Italian plum tomatoes,
roughly chopped
1 garlic clove, roughly chopped
about 750ml/1¼ pints/3 cups chicken or
vegetable stock
120ml/4fl oz/½ cup dry white wine
30ml/2 tbsp sun-dried tomato paste
30ml/2 tbsp shredded fresh basil, plus a
few whole leaves to garnish
30ml/2 tbsp single (light) cream
salt and ground black pepper

SERVES 4

1 Heat the olive oil in a large pan over a medium heat. Add the chopped onion and cook gently for about 5 minutes, stirring frequently, until it is softened but not brown.

NUTRITIONAL NOTES
Per portion:

Energy	77Kcals/324kJ
Total fat	3.9g
Saturated fat	1.1g
Cholesterol	2.74mg
Fibre	1.75g

4 Add the cream to the soup in the pan and heat through, stirring. Do not allow the soup to boil. Check the consistency of the soup and add more hot stock if necessary, then adjust the seasoning. Pour into soup bowls and garnish with whole basil leaves. Serve at once.

WILD MUSHROOM SOUP

Dried porcini mushrooms have an intense flavour so only a small quantity is needed for this
delicious soup. The beef stock helps to strengthen the earthy flavour of the mushrooms.

INGREDIENTS

25g/1oz/¹/2 cup dried porcini mushrooms
15ml/1 tbsp olive oil
2 leeks, thinly sliced
2 shallots, roughly chopped
1 garlic clove, roughly chopped
225g/8oz/3 cups fresh wild mushrooms
1.2 litres/2 pints/5 cups beef stock
2.5ml/¹/2 tsp dried thyme
30ml/2 tbsp single (light) cream
salt and ground black pepper
fresh thyme sprigs, to garnish

SERVES 4

1 Put the dried porcini in a bowl, add
250ml/8fl oz/1 cup warm water and leave
to soak for 20–30 minutes. Lift out of the
liquid and squeeze over the bowl to
remove as much of the soaking liquid as
possible. Strain all the liquid and reserve
to use later. Finely chop the porcini and
set aside.

2 Heat the olive oil in a large pan.
Add the leeks, shallots and garlic and
cook gently for about 5 minutes, stirring
the mixture frequently, until softened
but not coloured.

3 Chop or slice the fresh mushrooms and
add to the pan. Stir over a medium heat
for a few minutes until they begin to
soften. Pour in the beef stock and bring to
the boil. Add the chopped porcini,
reserved soaking liquid, dried thyme and
salt and pepper. Reduce the heat, half
cover the pan and simmer gently for
30 minutes, stirring occasionally.

4 Pour about three-quarters of the soup
into a blender or food processor and
blend until smooth. Return to the soup
remaining in the pan, stir in the cream
and heat through gently. Check the
consistency and add more stock if the
soup is too thick. Adjust the seasoning.
Serve hot in soup bowls, garnished with
fresh thyme sprigs.

NUTRITIONAL NOTES
Per portion:

Energy	66Kcals/276kJ
Total fat	4.7g
Saturated fat	1.2g
Cholesterol	3.32mg
Fibre	1.2g

PASTA AND CHICKPEA SOUP

—

A simple, country-style soup, ideal for a flavourful, low-fat appetizer. You can use other pasta
shapes, but conchiglie are ideal because they scoop up the chickpeas and beans.

INGREDIENTS

1 onion
2 carrots
2 celery sticks
15ml/1 tbsp olive oil
400g/14oz can chickpeas, rinsed and drained
*200g/7oz can cannellini beans, rinsed
and drained*
*150ml/1/4 pint/2/3 cup passata (bottled
strained tomatoes)*
120ml/4fl oz/1/2 cup water
*1.5 litres/21/2 pints/61/4 cups vegetable or
chicken stock*
1 fresh or dried rosemary sprig
200g/7oz/scant 2 cups dried conchiglie
salt and ground black pepper
fresh rosemary leaves, to garnish
*15ml/1 tbsp freshly grated Parmesan
cheese, to serve*

SERVES 6

1 Chop the onion, carrots and celery
sticks finely, either in a food processor or
by hand.

2 Heat the olive oil in a large, heavy pan,
add the chopped vegetables and cook
over a low heat, stirring frequently, for
5–7 minutes.

3 Add the chickpeas and cannellini
beans, stir well to mix, then cook for
5 minutes. Stir in the passata and water.
Cook, stirring, for 2–3 minutes.

4 Add 475ml/16fl oz/2 cups of the stock,
the rosemary sprig and salt and pepper to
taste. Bring to the boil, cover, then
simmer gently, stirring occasionally, for
1 hour.

NUTRITIONAL NOTES
Per portion:

Energy	201Kcals/849kJ
Total fat	4.5g
Saturated fat	0.9g
Cholesterol	1.84mg
Fibre	3.4g

5 Pour in the remaining stock, add the
pasta and bring to the boil, stirring.
Reduce the heat and simmer, stirring
frequently for 7–8 minutes, or according
to the packet instructions, until the
pasta is tender or *al dente*. Adjust the
seasoning. Remove and discard the
rosemary sprig and serve the hot soup in
soup bowls, topped with a few rosemary
leaves and a little grated Parmesan.

MINESTRONE

Root vegetables form the basis of this low-fat, chunky soup. For a more substantial meal,
serve with fresh crusty bread.

INGREDIENTS

15ml/1 tbsp olive oil
1 onion, roughly chopped
3 carrots, cut into large chunks
*175–200g/6–7oz turnips, cut into
large chunks*
*175g/6oz swede (rutabaga), cut into
large chunks*
400g/14oz can chopped Italian tomatoes
15ml/1 tbsp tomato purée (paste)
5ml/1 tsp dried mixed herbs
5ml/1 tsp dried oregano
*50g/2oz/1/2 cup dried (bell) peppers,
washed and thinly sliced (optional)*
*1.5 litres/2 1/2 pints/6 1/4 cups vegetable
stock or water*
50g/2oz/1/2 cup dried small macaroni
*400g/14oz can red kidney beans, rinsed
and drained*
30ml/2 tbsp chopped fresh flat leaf parsley
salt and ground black pepper
*15ml/1 tbsp freshly grated Parmesan
cheese, to serve*

SERVES 6

1 Heat the oil in a large pan, add the onion and cook over a low heat for about 5 minutes until softened. Add the prepared fresh vegetables, canned tomatoes, tomato purée, dried herbs and dried peppers, if using. Stir in salt and pepper to taste. Pour in the stock or water and bring to the boil. Stir well, cover, reduce the heat and simmer for 30 minutes, stirring occasionally.

2 Add the pasta and bring to the boil, stirring, then simmer, uncovered, for about 5 minutes or according to the packet instructions, until the pasta is just tender or *al dente*. Stir frequently.

3 Stir in the beans. Heat through for 2–3 minutes, then remove from the heat and stir in the parsley. Adjust the seasoning. Serve hot in soup bowls, sprinkled with a little grated Parmesan.

COOK'S TIP

Dried Italian peppers are piquant and firm with a "meaty" bite, which makes them ideal for adding substance to vegetarian soups.

NUTRITIONAL NOTES

Per portion:

Energy	159Kcals/671kJ
Total fat	4g
Saturated fat	0.9g
Cholesterol	2.36mg
Fibre	6.6g

LENTIL SOUP WITH TOMATOES

This classic rustic Italian soup is low in fat and flavoured with rosemary, and is delicious served
with plain crusty bread or low-fat garlic bread.

INGREDIENTS

*225g/8oz/1 cup dried green or
brown lentils
10ml/2 tsp extra virgin olive oil
2 rindless lean back bacon rashers (strips),
cut into small dice
1 onion, finely chopped
2 celery sticks, finely chopped
2 carrots, finely diced
2 fresh rosemary sprigs, finely chopped
2 bay leaves
400g/14oz can chopped plum tomatoes
1.75 litres/3 pints/7 1/2 cups vegetable stock
salt and ground black pepper
fresh bay leaves and rosemary sprigs,
to garnish*

SERVES 4

1 Place the lentils in a bowl and cover
with cold water. Leave to soak for 2 hours.
Rinse and drain well.

2 Heat the oil in a large pan. Add the
bacon and cook for about 3 minutes, then
stir in the chopped onion and cook for 5
minutes until softened, stirring
occasionally. Stir in the celery, carrots,
chopped rosemary, bay leaves and lentils.

3 Add the tomatoes and stock and bring
to the boil. Reduce the heat, half-cover
the pan, and simmer for about 1 hour, or
until the lentils are perfectly tender,
stirring occasionally.

4 Remove and discard the bay leaves,
add salt and pepper to taste and serve
garnished with bay leaves and rosemary.

NUTRITIONAL NOTES
Per portion:

Energy	235Kcals/995kJ
Total fat	4.9g
Saturated fat	0.9g
Cholesterol	3.48mg
Fibre	6.9g

SPINACH AND RICE SOUP

Use very fresh, young spinach leaves to prepare this light and fresh-tasting low-fat Italian soup.

INGREDIENTS

*675g/1 1/2lb fresh spinach, washed
15ml/1 tbsp extra virgin olive oil
1 small onion, finely chopped
2 garlic cloves, finely chopped
1 small fresh red chilli, deseeded and
finely chopped
115g/4oz/generous 1/2 cup risotto rice
1.2 litres/2 pints/5 cups vegetable stock
salt and freshly ground black pepper
20ml/4 tsp freshly grated Pecorino cheese,
to serve*

SERVES 4

1 Place the spinach in a large pan with
just the water clinging to the leaves. Add
a large pinch of salt and heat gently until
wilted. Remove from the heat and drain,
reserving any liquid.

2 Either chop the spinach finely or place
in a food processor and blend to a purée.

3 Heat the oil in a pan and cook the
onion, garlic and chilli for 4–5 minutes,
stirring occasionally. Stir in the rice, then
the stock and spinach liquid. Boil, then
simmer for 10 minutes. Add the spinach
and seasoning and cook for 5–7 minutes.
Serve with the Pecorino cheese.

NUTRITIONAL NOTES
Per portion:

Energy	235Kcals/995kJ
Total fat	4.9g
Saturated fat	0.9g
Cholesterol	3.48mg
Fibre	6.9g

FARFALLE SALAD WITH PIQUANT PEPPERS

Peppers, pasta and fresh coriander add delicious flavour to this quick and easy
Italian appetizer or supper dish.

INGREDIENTS

1 red, 1 yellow and 1 orange (bell) pepper
1 garlic clove, crushed
30ml/2 tbsp capers
30ml/2 tbsp raisins
5ml/1 tsp wholegrain mustard
finely grated rind and juice of 1 lime
5ml/1 tsp clear honey
30ml/2 tbsp chopped fresh
coriander (cilantro)
225g/8oz/2 cups dried farfalle
salt and ground black pepper
freshly shaved Parmesan cheese, to serve

SERVES 8

1 Quarter the peppers and remove and
discard the stalk and seeds. Put into a
pan of boiling water and cook for about
10–15 minutes until tender. Drain and
rinse under cold water. Drain again. Peel
off and discard the skin and cut the flesh
into strips lengthwise. Set aside.

NUTRITIONAL NOTES
Per portion:

Energy	160Kcals/681kJ
Total fat	1g
Saturated fat	0.2g
Cholesterol	0mg
Fibre	1.9g

2 Put the garlic, capers, raisins, mustard,
lime rind and juice, honey, coriander and
seasoning to taste into a bowl and whisk
together. Set aside.

VARIATION
If you prefer, make this salad with only
one colour of pepper. The green ones are
too bitter, however, and are not suitable.

3 Cook the pasta in a large pan of
boiling, salted water for 10–12 minutes
until tender or *al dente*. Drain.

4 Return the pasta to the pan, add the
reserved peppers and dressing. Heat
gently and toss to mix. Transfer to a warm
serving bowl and serve immediately.
Sprinkle with a few shavings of Parmesan
cheese to taste.

ARTICHOKE SALAD WITH SALSA AGRODOLCE

Agrodolce is an Italian sweet-and-sour sauce which makes an ideal accompaniment for this artichoke and bean salad.

INGREDIENTS

6 small globe artichokes
juice of 1 lemon
15ml/1 tbsp olive oil
2 onions, roughly chopped
175g/6oz/1 cup fresh or frozen broad
(fava) beans, shelled weight
175g/6oz/1¹/₂ cups fresh or frozen peas,
shelled weight
salt and ground black pepper
fresh mint leaves, to garnish

FOR THE SALSA AGRODOLCE

120ml/4fl oz/¹/₂ cup white wine vinegar
15ml/1 tbsp caster (superfine) sugar
handful of fresh mint leaves, roughly torn

SERVES 4–6

1 Peel and discard the outer leaves from the artichokes and cut into quarters. Place the artichokes in a bowl of water with the lemon juice.

2 Heat the oil in a large pan and add the onions. Cook until the onions are golden, stirring occasionally. Add the broad beans and stir, then drain the artichokes and add to the pan. Pour in about 300ml/¹/₂ pint/1¹/₄ cups of water, bring to the boil, then cook, covered, for 10–15 minutes.

3 Add the peas, season with salt and pepper and cook for a further 5 minutes, stirring occasionally, until the vegetables are tender. Strain through a sieve, discard the liquid, then place all the vegetables in a bowl, leave to cool, cover and chill.

4 To make the salsa, mix the ingredients in a pan. Heat gently for 2–3 minutes until the sugar has dissolved, then simmer for a further 5 minutes, stirring occasionally. Remove from the heat and let cool. To serve, drizzle over the vegetables and garnish with mint leaves.

NUTRITIONAL NOTES
Per portion:

Energy	182Kcals/759kJ
Total fat	4g
Saturated fat	0.6g
Cholesterol	0mg
Fibre	5.5g

ROCKET, PEAR AND PARMESAN SALAD

For a sophisticated start to a meal with friends, try this simple Italian salad of fresh, ripe pears, tasty Parmesan and aromatic leaves of rocket. Serve with fresh Italian bread or crispbreads.

INGREDIENTS

*3 ripe pears, such as Williams
or Packhams
10ml/2 tsp lemon juice
15ml/1 tbsp hazelnut or walnut oil
115g/4oz rocket (arugula)
25g/1oz fresh Parmesan cheese
ground black pepper*

SERVES 4

1 Peel and core the pears and slice thickly. Place in a bowl and moisten with lemon juice to keep the flesh white.

2 Combine the nut oil with the pears. Add the rocket leaves and toss to mix.

3 Divide the salad among four small plates and top each portion with shavings of Parmesan cheese. Season with ground black pepper and serve.

COOK'S TIP
You can grow your own rocket from early spring to late summer. You can also use watercress instead.

NUTRITIONAL NOTES
Per portion:

Energy	102Kcals/424kJ
Total fat	5g
Saturated fat	1.6g
Cholesterol	6.24mg
Fibre	2.6g

MELON, PROSCIUTTO AND STRAWBERRY SALAD

—

Sections of cool fragrant melon wrapped with thin slices of air-dried Italian ham make this
delicious Italian salad or snack.

INGREDIENTS
*1 large melon, such as cantaloupe, Galia
or Charentais
115g/4oz prosciutto or Serrano ham,
thinly sliced*

FOR THE SALSA
*225g/8oz strawberries
5ml/1 tsp caster (superfine) sugar
20ml/4 tsp groundnut (peanut) or
sunflower oil
15ml/1 tbsp unsweetened orange juice
2.5ml/¹/₂ tsp finely grated orange rind
2.5ml/¹/₂ tsp finely grated fresh root ginger
salt and ground black pepper*

SERVES 4

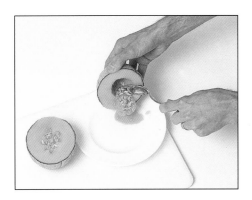

1 Halve the melon and remove the seeds
with a spoon. Cut the rind away with a
paring knife. Discard the seeds and rind,
then slice the melon flesh thickly. Chill
until ready to serve.

2 To make the salsa, hull the strawberries
and cut them into large dice. Place in a
small mixing bowl with the sugar and
crush lightly to release the juices. Add
the oil, orange juice, orange rind and
ginger. Season with salt and a generous
twist of black pepper.

3 Arrange the melon on a serving plate,
lay the ham over the top and serve with
the bowl of salsa alongside.

NUTRITIONAL NOTES
Per portion:

Energy	89Kcals/369kJ
Total fat	4.9g
Saturated fat	0.8g
Cholesterol	13.66mg
Fibre	0.8g

COOK'S TIP
Melon has a very subtle flavour. To
enjoy it at its best, do not over-chill it.

THREE-COLOUR SALAD

This classic Italian dish, *insalata tricolore*, creates a tasty and colourful appetizer
or snack. Use plum or vine-ripened tomatoes for the best flavour.

INGREDIENTS
1 small red onion, thinly sliced
6 large full-flavoured tomatoes
50g/2oz/1 small bunch rocket (arugula) or
watercress, roughly chopped
115g/4oz reduced-fat mozzarella cheese,
thinly sliced or grated
20ml/4 tsp extra virgin olive oil
30ml/2 tbsp pine nuts (optional)
salt and ground black pepper

SERVES 6

2 Prepare the tomatoes for skinning by slashing them with a sharp knife and dipping briefly in boiling water.

3 Peel off the skins and then slice each tomato using a sharp knife.

4 Arrange half the tomato slices on a large platter, or divide them among six small plates if you prefer.

5 Layer with half the chopped rocket or watercress and half the onion slices, seasoning well. Add half the cheese, sprinkling over a little more seasoning as you go.

6 Repeat with the remaining tomato and onion slices, salad leaves and cheese.

7 Season well to finish and sprinkle the oil over the salad. Scatter the pine nuts over the top, if using. Cover the salad and chill for at least 2 hours before serving.

VARIATIONS
Instead of the fresh rocket or watercress, use chopped fresh basil, which goes particularly well with the flavour of ripe tomatoes. To reduce the fat content even further, omit the oil and sprinkle the salad with a fat-free vinaigrette dressing.

1 Soak the onion slices in a bowl of cold water for 30 minutes, then drain and pat dry.

NUTRITIONAL NOTES
Per portion:

Energy	75Kcals/314kJ
Total fat	5g
Saturated fat	2g
Cholesterol	7.36mg
Fibre	0.6g

ROASTED PEPPER AND TOMATO SALAD

This recipe brings together perfectly the colours, flavours and textures of southern Italian food.
Serve this low-fat dish at room temperature with a green salad.

INGREDIENTS

3 red (bell) peppers
6 large plum tomatoes
2.5ml/¹/2 tsp dried red chilli flakes
1 red onion, thinly sliced
3 garlic cloves, finely chopped
finely grated rind and juice of 1 lemon
45ml/3 tbsp chopped fresh flat leaf parsley
20ml/4 tsp extra virgin olive oil
salt and ground black pepper
25g/1oz black and green olives and extra
chopped fresh flat leaf parsley, to garnish

SERVES 4

1 Preheat the oven to 220°C/425°F/Gas 7. Place the peppers on a baking sheet and roast in the oven, turning occasionally, for 10 minutes or until the skins are almost blackened. Add the tomatoes to the baking sheet and bake for a further 5 minutes.

2 Place the peppers in a plastic bag, close the top loosely, trapping in the steam, and then set them aside with the tomatoes until they are cool enough to handle.

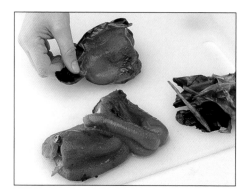

3 Carefully pull off and discard the skin from the peppers. Remove and discard the seeds, then chop the peppers and tomatoes roughly and place them together in a mixing bowl.

4 Add the chilli flakes, onion, garlic, lemon rind and juice. Sprinkle over the parsley. Mix well, then transfer to a serving dish. Sprinkle with a little salt and black pepper, drizzle over the olive oil and sprinkle the olives and extra parsley over the top to garnish. Serve the salad at room temperature.

NUTRITIONAL NOTES
Per portion:

Energy	78Kcals/323kJ
Total fat	4.9g
Saturated fat	0.8g
Cholesterol	0mg
Fibre	2.1g

MARINATED COURGETTES

This is a simple vegetable dish which is prepared all over Italy using the best of the season's
courgettes. It can be eaten hot or cold and creates a delicious accompaniment to a main course.

INGREDIENTS

4 courgettes (zucchini)
40ml/8 tsp extra virgin olive oil
30ml/2 tbsp chopped fresh mint, plus
whole leaves, to garnish
30ml/2 tbsp white wine vinegar
salt and ground black pepper

SERVES 6

1 Cut the courgettes into thin slices. Heat 20ml/4 tsp of the oil in a wide, heavy pan.

2 Fry the courgettes in batches, for 4–6 minutes, until tender and brown around the edges. Transfer the courgettes to a bowl. Season well.

NUTRITIONAL NOTES
Per portion:

Energy	50Kcals/206KJ
Total fat	5.0g
Saturated fat	0.7g
Cholesterol	0mg
Fibre	0.3g

3 Heat the remaining oil, then add the mint and vinegar and let bubble for a few seconds. Stir into the courgettes. Marinate for 1 hour, then serve with mint leaves.

ROASTED PLUM TOMATOES WITH GARLIC

A very typical Italian dish, these roast tomatoes flavoured with garlic are so simple to prepare, yet taste absolutely wonderful. A shallow earthenware dish will allow the tomatoes to char.

INGREDIENTS

8 plum tomatoes
12 garlic cloves
20ml/4 tsp extra virgin olive oil
3 bay leaves
salt and ground black pepper
45ml/3 tbsp fresh oregano leaves,
to garnish

SERVES 4

1 Preheat the oven to 230°C/450°F/Gas 8. Cut the plum tomatoes in half, leaving a small part of the green stem intact for the final decoration.

2 Select an ovenproof dish that will hold all the tomatoes snugly together in a single layer. Place them in the dish with the cut side facing upwards, and push each of the whole, unpeeled garlic cloves among them.

3 Lightly brush the tomatoes with the oil, add the bay leaves and sprinkle black pepper over the top.

4 Bake in the oven for about 35–45 minutes until the tomatoes have softened and are sizzling in the dish. They should be charred around the edges. Season with salt and a little more black pepper, if needed. Garnish with the fresh oregano leaves and serve immediately.

COOK'S TIP

Select ripe, juicy tomatoes without any blemishes to get the best flavour.

VARIATION

For a sweet alternative, use halved and seeded red or yellow (bell) peppers instead of the tomatoes.

NUTRITIONAL NOTES
Per portion:

Energy	57Kcals/238kJ
Total fat	4.0g
Saturated fat	0.6g
Cholesterol	0mg
Fibre	1.1g

PROSCIUTTO AND PEPPER PIZZAS

The delicious flavours of these quick and easy Italian pizza snacks are hard to beat.
Serve with mixed salad leaves and sliced plum tomatoes.

INGREDIENTS
1/2 loaf of ciabatta bread
1 red (bell) pepper, roasted, peeled
and deseeded
1 yellow (bell) pepper, roasted, peeled
and deseeded
4 thin slices prosciutto, cut into
thick strips
50g/2oz reduced-fat mozzarella cheese
ground black pepper
tiny fresh basil leaves,
to garnish

MAKES 4

3 Thinly slice the mozzarella and arrange on top, then grind over plenty of black pepper. Grill (broil) for 2–3 minutes until the cheese is bubbling.

NUTRITIONAL NOTES
Per portion:

Energy	213Kcals/903kJ
Total fat	3.9g
Saturated fat	1.67g
Cholesterol	8.76mg
Fibre	1.5

4 Sprinkle the basil leaves on top to garnish and serve immediately.

1 Cut the bread into four thick slices and toast until golden.

2 Cut the roasted peppers into thick strips and arrange on the toasted bread with the strips of prosciutto. Preheat the grill (broiler).

MEAT
AND
POULTRY

By choosing LEAN CUTS *of meat
and poultry, these foods can be* ENJOYED
as part of a HEALTHY *low-fat diet.
Choose from this nourishing collection of
low-fat Italian* MAIN COURSE *meat and
poultry dishes, including a* LOW-FAT
Lasagne, Tuscan Chicken and VEAL *with
Tomatoes and White* WINE.

FILLET OF BEEF WITH HERBY TAGLIATELLE

This Italian-style fillet of beef served with herby pasta creates a delicious
low-fat main course or supper dish.

INGREDIENTS

450g/1lb lean beef fillet (tenderloin)
450g/1lb fresh tagliatelle made with
sun-dried tomatoes and herbs
115g/4oz cherry tomatoes
1/2 cucumber

FOR THE MARINADE

15ml/1 tbsp soy sauce
15ml/1 tbsp sherry
5ml/1 tsp fresh root ginger, peeled
and grated
1 garlic clove, crushed

FOR THE HERB DRESSING

150ml/1/4 pint/2/3 cup low-fat
natural (plain) yogurt
1 garlic clove, crushed
30–45ml/2–3 tbsp chopped fresh herbs
such as chives, parsley and thyme
salt and ground black pepper

SERVES 6

1 Mix all the marinade ingredients together in a shallow non-metallic dish, put the beef in and turn it over to coat it. Cover with clear film (plastic wrap) and leave for 30 minutes to allow the flavours to penetrate the meat.

2 Preheat the grill (broiler). Remove the fillet from the marinade, pat dry with kitchen paper and grill on a rack for 8 minutes on each side, basting with the marinade.

3 Transfer to a plate, cover with foil and leave to stand for 20 minutes.

4 Mix the dressing ingredients thoroughly. Cook the pasta in a large pan of lightly salted boiling water, according to the packet instructions, until tender or *al dente*. Drain thoroughly, rinse under cold water and drain again.

5 Cut the cherry tomatoes in half. Cut the cucumber in half lengthwise, scoop out and discard the seeds with a teaspoon and slice the flesh thinly into crescents.

6 Put the pasta, cherry tomatoes, cucumber and dressing into a bowl and toss to mix well. Slice the beef thinly and arrange on serving plates with the pasta salad served alongside.

NUTRITIONAL NOTES

Per portion:

Energy	201Kcals/848kJ
Total fat	4.3g
Saturated fat	1.7g
Cholesterol	45.25mg
Fibre	1.2g

BEEF STEW WITH TOMATOES, WINE AND PEAS

—

This is a traditional Italian recipe known as *spezzatino* which is perfect for a winter lunch or
dinner. Serve it with boiled or mashed potatoes to soak up the delicious sauce.

INGREDIENTS

30ml/2 tbsp plain (all-purpose) flour
10ml/2 tsp chopped fresh thyme or 5ml/
1 tsp dried thyme
450g/1lb lean braising or stewing beef,
cut into cubes
10ml/2 tsp olive oil
2 onions, roughly chopped
450g/1lb jar sugocasa or passata (bottle
strained tomatoes)
250ml/8fl oz/1 cup beef stock
250ml/8fl oz/1 cup red wine
2 garlic cloves, crushed
30ml/2 tbsp tomato purée (paste)
275g/10oz/2½ cups shelled fresh peas
5ml/1 tsp sugar
salt and ground black pepper
fresh thyme sprigs, to garnish

SERVES 6

1 Preheat the oven to 160°C/325°F/Gas 3.
Put the flour in a shallow dish and season
with the chopped thyme and salt and
pepper. Add the beef cubes and turn to
coat evenly with the flour.

VARIATION
Use thawed frozen peas instead of
fresh. Add them 10 minutes before the
end of cooking.

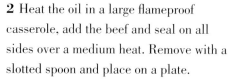

2 Heat the oil in a large flameproof
casserole, add the beef and seal on all
sides over a medium heat. Remove with a
slotted spoon and place on a plate.

3 Add the onion to the pan, scraping the
base of the pan to mix in any sediment.
Cook gently for 3 minutes, stirring
frequently, then stir in the sugocasa or
passata, stock, wine, garlic and tomato
purée. Bring to the boil, stirring. Return
the beef to the pan and stir well to coat
with the sauce. Cover and cook in the
oven for 1½ hours.

4 Stir in the peas and sugar. Re-cover,
return the casserole to the oven and cook
for a further 30 minutes, or until the beef
is tender. Adjust the seasoning to taste.
Garnish with fresh thyme sprigs and
serve immediately.

NUTRITIONAL NOTES
Per portion:

Energy	183Kcals/768kJ
Total fat	4.9g
Saturated fat	1.5g
Cholesterol	38.3mg
Fibre	2.8g

CALF'S LIVER WITH BALSAMIC VINEGAR

This delicious sweet-and-sour liver dish is a speciality of Venice. Serve it very simply, with green
beans sprinkled with toasted fresh breadcrumbs, for an appetizing supper dish.

2 Heat the oil in a wide, heavy pan.
Add the onion rings and cook gently,
stirring frequently, for about 5 minutes
until softened but not coloured. Remove
with a fish slice (spatula), place on a
plate and set aside.

3 Add the coated liver to the juices in the
pan and cook over a medium heat for
2–3 minutes on each side. Transfer to
warmed serving plates and keep hot.

4 Add the wine and vinegar to the pan
and stir to mix with the pan juices and
any sediment. Add the onions and sugar
and heat through until hot and bubbling,
stirring constantly. Spoon the sauce over
the liver, garnish with fresh sage sprigs
and serve immediately.

INGREDIENTS

15ml/1 tbsp plain (all-purpose) flour
2.5ml/¹/2 tsp finely chopped fresh sage
4 thin slices calf's liver, cut into
serving pieces
15ml/1 tbsp olive oil
2 small red onions, sliced and separated
into rings
150ml/¹/4 pint/²/3 cup dry white wine
45ml/3 tbsp balsamic vinegar
pinch of sugar
salt and ground black pepper
fresh sage sprigs, to garnish

SERVES 4

1 Spread out the flour in a shallow bowl.
Season it with the chopped sage and
plenty of salt and pepper. Add the liver
and turn it in the flour until well coated.

NUTRITIONAL NOTES
Per portion:

Energy	110Kcals/457kJ
Total fat	4.9g
Saturated fat	1g
Cholesterol	102.85mg
Fibre	0.3g

VEAL WITH TOMATOES AND WHITE WINE

—

Known as *Osso Buco*, this delicious dish is traditionally served with Milanese Risotto. The zesty
gremolata garnish adds a refreshing taste to this hearty dish.

INGREDIENTS

30ml/2 tbsp plain (all-purpose) flour
4 pieces of lean veal shank
2 small onions
10ml/2 tsp olive oil
1 large celery stick,
finely chopped
1 carrot, finely chopped
2 garlic cloves, finely chopped
400g/14oz can chopped tomatoes
300ml/1/2 pint/11/4 cups dry
white wine
300ml/1/2 pint/11/4 cups chicken or
veal stock
1 strip of thinly pared lemon rind
2 bay leaves, plus extra to garnish
salt and ground black pepper

FOR THE GREMOLATA

30ml/2 tbsp finely chopped fresh flat
leaf parsley
finely grated rind of 1 lemon
1 garlic clove, finely chopped

SERVES 4

1 Preheat the oven to 160°C/325°F/Gas 3.
Season the flour with salt and pepper and
spread it out in a shallow bowl. Add the
pieces of veal and turn them in the flour
until they are evenly coated. Shake off
any excess flour.

2 Slice one of the onions into rings. Heat
the olive oil in a large flameproof
casserole, then add the veal pieces, with
the onion rings, and brown the veal on
both sides over a medium heat. Remove
the veal with tongs, place on a plate and
set aside to drain.

3 Chop the remaining onion and add to
the pan with the celery, carrot and garlic.
Stir the bottom of the pan to mix in the
juices and sediment. Cook gently, stirring
frequently, for about 5 minutes until the
vegetables soften slightly.

4 Add the tomatoes, wine, stock, lemon
rind and bay leaves, then season to taste
with salt and pepper. Bring the mixture to
the boil, stirring.

5 Return the veal pieces to the pan and
stir to coat thoroughly with the sauce.
Cover and cook in the oven for 2 hours or
until the veal feels tender when pierced
with a fork.

6 Meanwhile, make the gremolata. Mix
together the parsley, lemon rind and
garlic in a small bowl. Remove the
casserole from the oven and discard the
lemon rind and bay leaves. Adjust the
seasoning. Serve hot, sprinkled with the
gremolata and garnished with bay leaves.

NUTRITIONAL NOTES
Per portion:

Energy	219Kcals/919kJ
Total fat	4.8g
Saturated fat	1.2g
Cholesterol	84.8mg
Fibre	1.3g

PANCETTA AND BEAN RISOTTO

This delicious Italian risotto makes a healthy and filling low-fat meal, served with cooked fresh
seasonal vegetables or a mixed green salad.

INGREDIENTS
10ml/2 tsp olive oil
1 onion, chopped
2 garlic cloves, finely chopped
115g/4oz smoked pancetta, diced
350g/12oz/1¾ cups risotto rice
*1.5 litres/2½ pints/6¼ cups simmering
chicken stock*
*225g/8oz/1⅓ cups frozen baby broad
(fava) beans*
*30ml/2 tbsp chopped fresh mixed herbs,
such as parsley, thyme and oregano*
salt and ground black pepper
*freshly shaved Parmesan cheese,
to serve (optional)*

SERVES 6

1 Heat the oil in a large pan. Add the
onion, garlic and pancetta and cook
gently for about 5 minutes, stirring
occasionally. Do not allow the onion and
garlic to brown.

2 Add the rice and cook for 1 minute,
stirring. Add a ladleful of stock and
cook, stirring, until absorbed.

3 Add more ladlefuls of stock until the
rice is tender and almost all the liquid
absorbed. This will take 30–35 minutes.
Meanwhile, cook the broad beans in
salted, boiling water for about 3 minutes.
Drain and stir into the risotto, with the
herbs. Season to taste. Sprinkle with
shavings of Parmesan cheese, if using.

NUTRITIONAL NOTES
Per portion:

Energy	294Kcals/1250kJ
Total fat	5g
Saturated fat	1.6g
Cholesterol	8.5mg
Fibre	2.7g

HUNTER'S CHICKEN

This traditional Italian dish combines chicken with a flavourful tomato, mushroom and herb
sauce to create a tempting main course, ideal served with mashed potatoes or cooked polenta.

3 Add the onion and chopped porcini
mushrooms to the pan. Cook gently,
stirring frequently, for about 3 minutes
until the onion has softened but not
browned. Stir in the chopped tomatoes,
wine and reserved mushroom soaking
liquid, then add the crushed garlic and
chopped rosemary, with salt and black
pepper to taste. Bring to the boil,
stirring constantly.

4 Return the chicken to the pan and
turn to coat it with the sauce. Cover
and simmer gently for 30 minutes.

5 Add the fresh mushrooms and stir
well to mix into the sauce. Continue
simmering gently for 10 minutes or
until the chicken is tender. Adjust the
seasoning to taste. Serve hot, garnished
with fresh rosemary sprigs.

INGREDIENTS

15g/1/2oz/1/4 cup dried porcini mushrooms
10ml/2 tsp olive oil
4 small chicken portions, on the
bone, skinned
1 large onion, thinly sliced
400g/14oz can chopped tomatoes
150ml/1/4 pint/2/3 cup red wine
1 garlic clove, crushed
leaves of 1 sprig of fresh rosemary,
finely chopped
115g/4oz/1 3/4 cups fresh field (portabello)
mushrooms, thinly sliced
salt and ground black pepper
fresh rosemary sprigs, to garnish

SERVES 4

1 Put the porcini in a bowl, add 250ml/
8fl oz/1 cup warm water and leave to
soak for 20–30 minutes. Remove from
the liquid and squeeze over the bowl.
Strain the liquid and reserve. Finely chop
the porcini.

2 Heat the oil in a large flameproof
casserole. Add the chicken. Sauté over a
medium heat for 5 minutes, or until
golden. Remove and drain on absorbent
kitchen paper.

NUTRITIONAL NOTES
Per portion:

Energy	190Kcals/801kJ
Total fat	5g
Saturated fat	1.3g
Cholesterol	44.12mg
Fibre	1.2g

TUSCAN CHICKEN

This simple Italian peasant casserole has all the flavours of traditional Tuscan ingredients and creates a delicious, low-fat supper dish.

3 Lower the heat and simmer gently, stirring occasionally, for 30–35 minutes or until the chicken is tender and the juices run clear, not pink, when pierced with the point of a knife.

4 Stir in the cannellini beans and simmer for a further 5 minutes until heated through. Sprinkle with the breadcrumbs and cook under a hot grill (broiler) until golden brown. Serve immediately, garnished with fresh oregano sprigs.

INGREDIENTS
8 chicken thighs, skinned
5ml/1 tsp olive oil
1 onion, thinly sliced
2 red (bell) peppers, deseeded and sliced
1 garlic clove, crushed
300ml/¹/₂ pint/1¹/₄ cups passata (bottled strained tomatoes)
150ml/¹/₄ pint/²/₃ cup dry white wine
a large sprig of fresh oregano, chopped, or 5ml/1 tsp dried oregano
400g/14oz can cannellini beans, drained
45ml/3 tbsp fresh breadcrumbs
salt and ground black pepper
fresh oregano sprigs, to garnish

SERVES 6

1 Fry the chicken in the oil in a non-stick or heavy pan until golden brown all over. Remove from the pan, place on a plate and keep hot. Add the onion and peppers to the pan and gently sauté until softened, but not brown. Add the garlic.

2 Add the chicken, passata, wine and oregano and stir. Season well and bring to the boil, stirring, then cover the pan tightly.

NUTRITIONAL NOTES
Per portion:

Energy	256Kcals/1083kJ
Total fat	4.8g
Saturated fat	1.3g
Cholesterol	49.3mg
Fibre	1.1g

CHICKEN IN A SALT CRUST

Cooking food in a casing of salt gives a deliciously moist, tender flavour that, surprisingly, is not too salty. Serve with a selection of cooked fresh seasonal vegetables.

INGREDIENTS

1.75kg/4–4¹/2lb chicken
about 2.25kg/5¹/4lb coarse sea salt

SERVES 6

1 Preheat the oven to 220°C/425°F/Gas 7. Choose a deep ovenproof dish into which the whole chicken will fit snugly. Line the dish with a double thickness of heavy foil, allowing plenty of foil to overhang it.

2 Truss the chicken tightly so that the salt cannot fall into the cavity. Place the chicken on a thin layer of salt in the dish.

COOK'S TIP

This recipe makes a stunning and unusual main course. Garnish the salt-encrusted chicken with fresh mixed herbs and take to the table. Scrape away the salt and transfer to a clean plate to carve.

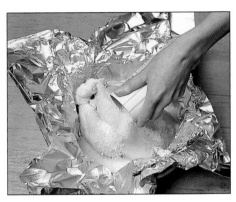

3 Pour the remaining salt all around and over the top of the chicken until it is completely encased. Sprinkle the top with a little water.

4 Cover tightly with the foil and bake the chicken on the lower shelf in the oven for 1³/4 hours until the chicken is cooked and tender.

5 To serve the chicken, open out the foil and ease it out of the dish. Place on a large serving platter. Crack open the salt crust on the chicken and brush away the salt. Remove and discard the skin from the chicken and carve the meat into slices. Serve.

NUTRITIONAL NOTES

Per portion:

Energy	156Kcals/659kJ
Total fat	4.4g
Saturated fat	1.3g
Cholesterol	61.6mg
Fibre	0g

TAGLIATELLE WITH RAGÙ SAUCE

—

This is an authentic meat sauce from the city of Bologna in Emilia-Romagna. It is quite rich and very delicious, and is always served with tagliatelle, never with spaghetti.

INGREDIENTS
450g/1lb dried tagliatelle
salt and ground black pepper
freshly grated Parmesan cheese,
to serve (optional)

FOR THE RAGÙ SAUCE
1 onion
2 carrots
2 celery sticks
2 garlic cloves
15ml/1 tbsp olive oil
115g/4oz lean back bacon, diced
250g/9oz extra-lean minced (ground) beef
250g/9oz extra-lean minced (ground) pork
120ml/4fl oz/1/2 cup dry white wine
2 × 400g/14oz cans crushed Italian plum tomatoes
475–750ml/16fl oz–1 1/4 pints/2–3 cups beef stock

SERVES 8

1 Make the ragù. Chop all the fresh vegetables finely. Heat the oil in a large frying pan. Add the chopped vegetables and the bacon and cook over a medium heat, stirring frequently, for 10 minutes or until the vegetables have softened.

2 Add the minced beef and pork, reduce the heat and cook gently for 10 minutes, stirring frequently and breaking up any lumps in the meat with a wooden spoon.

3 Stir in salt and pepper to taste, then add the wine and stir again. Simmer for about 5 minutes, or until reduced.

4 Add the tomatoes and 250ml/8fl oz/ 1 cup of the stock and bring to the boil. Stir the sauce well, then reduce the heat. Half-cover the pan with a lid and leave to simmer very gently for 2 hours. Stir occasionally and add more stock as it becomes absorbed.

5 Simmer the sauce, without a lid, for a further 30 minutes, stirring frequently. Meanwhile, cook the pasta in a large pan of boiling salted water, according to the packet instructions, until tender or *al dente*. Taste the sauce and adjust the seasoning. Drain the cooked pasta and tip it into a warmed bowl. Pour the sauce over the pasta and toss well. Serve immediately, sprinkled with grated Parmesan, if using.

NUTRITIONAL NOTES
Per portion:

Energy	185Kcals/782kJ
Total fat	5g
Saturated fat	1.7g
Cholesterol	36.3mg
Fibre	1.8g

SPAGHETTI BOLOGNESE

A popular Italian dish, Spaghetti Bolognese is full of flavour and low in fat. In order to achieve
an even more full-flavoured sauce, some Italian cooks insist on cooking bolognese for 3–4 hours!

INGREDIENTS

10ml/2 tsp olive oil

1 onion, finely chopped

1 garlic clove, crushed

*450g/1lb extra-lean minced
(ground) turkey or beef*

*400g/14oz can chopped Italian
plum tomatoes*

*15ml/1 tbsp sun-dried tomato
purée (paste)*

5ml/1 tsp dried oregano

5ml/1 tsp dried basil

*450ml/¾ pint/scant 2 cups beef or
vegetable stock*

45ml/3 tbsp red wine

450g/1lb dried spaghetti

salt and ground black pepper

*25g/1oz freshly grated Parmesan cheese,
to serve (optional)*

SERVES 6

2 Stir in the tomatoes, sun-dried tomato
purée, oregano, basil and ground black
pepper. Pour in the stock and red wine
and bring to the boil, stirring. Season to
taste, cover the pan, reduce the heat and
leave the sauce to simmer for 1 hour,
stirring occasionally.

3 Meanwhile, cook the pasta in a large
pan of boiling salted water, according to
the packet instructions, until tender or *al
dente*. Drain, and divide among warmed
bowls. Taste the meat sauce and add more
salt if necessary, then spoon it on top of
the pasta and sprinkle with a little grated
Parmesan, if using. Serve immediately.

NUTRITIONAL NOTES

Per portion:

Energy	207Kcals/874kJ
Total fat	4.9g
Saturated fat	1.5g
Cholesterol	39.1mg
Fibre	1.8g

1 Heat the oil in a medium pan, add the
onion and garlic and cook over a low heat,
stirring frequently, for about 5 minutes
until softened. Add the minced beef or
turkey and cook gently for about
5 minutes, stirring frequently and
breaking up any lumps in the meat with
a wooden spoon.

SPAGHETTI WITH MEATBALLS

Italian-style meatballs simmered in a sweet and spicy tomato sauce are truly delicious served
with spaghetti, making an ideal low-fat dish for all the family to enjoy.

INGREDIENTS

60ml/4 tbsp fresh flat leaf parsley
350g/12oz extra-lean minced (ground) beef
1 egg
2.5ml/¹⁄2 tsp crushed dried red chillies
1 thick slice of white bread, crusts removed
30ml/2 tbsp semi-skimmed (low-fat) milk
15ml/1 tbsp olive oil
*300ml/¹⁄2 pint/1¹⁄4 cups passata (bottled
strained tomatoes)*
400ml/14fl oz/1²⁄3 cups vegetable stock
5ml/1 tsp sugar
450g/1lb dried spaghetti
salt and ground black pepper
*40g/1¹⁄2oz freshly grated Parmesan cheese,
to serve*

SERVES 8

1 Roughly chop the parsley. Mix half
with the minced beef, egg, and half the
crushed chillies in a large bowl. Season
with plenty of salt and pepper.

2 Tear the bread into small pieces and
place in a small bowl. Moisten with the
milk. Leave to soak for a few minutes,
then squeeze out and discard the excess
milk and crumble the bread over the meat
mixture. Mix everything together with a
wooden spoon, then use your hands to
squeeze and knead the mixture so that it
becomes smooth and quite sticky.

3 Wash your hands, rinse them under the
cold tap, then pick up small pieces of the
mixture and roll them between your
palms to make about 40–60 small balls.

4 Place the meatballs on a tray and chill
in the refrigerator for about 30 minutes.

5 Heat the oil in a large non-stick frying
pan. Cook the meatballs in batches until
browned all over. Set aside.

6 Pour the passata and stock into a large
pan. Heat gently, then add the remaining
chillies and the sugar, with salt and
pepper to taste. Add the meatballs to the
passata mixture, then bring to the boil.
Reduce the heat, cover and simmer for
20 minutes, stirring occasionally.

7 Cook the pasta in a large pan of boiling
salted water, according to the packet
instructions until it is tender or *al dente*.
Drain well and tip it into a warmed large
bowl. Pour the sauce over the pasta and
toss gently to mix. Sprinkle with the
remaining parsley and serve with freshly
grated Parmesan handed separately.

NUTRITIONAL NOTES
Per portion:

Energy	148Kcals/622kJ
Total fat	5g
Saturated fat	1.9g
Cholesterol	44.8mg
Fibre	0.9g

LAMB AND SWEET PEPPER SAUCE

This simple sauce is a speciality of the Abruzzo-Molise region of Italy, east of Rome, where it is
traditionally served with *maccheroni alla chitarra* – square-shaped long macaroni.

2 Sprinkle in the garlic and add the bay
leaves, then pour in the wine and let it
bubble until reduced.

INGREDIENTS

*250g/9oz boneless lean lamb neck
(shoulder or breast) fillet*
15ml/1 tbsp olive oil
2 garlic cloves, finely chopped
2 bay leaves, torn
250ml/8fl oz/1 cup dry white wine
*4 ripe Italian plum tomatoes, skinned
and chopped*
2 red (bell) peppers, deseeded and diced
450g/1lb dried spaghetti
salt and freshly ground black pepper

SERVES 6

1 Dice the lamb. Heat the oil in a
medium frying pan, add the lamb and
seasoning. Cook over a medium to high
heat for about 10 minutes, stirring
frequently, until browned all over.

3 Add the tomatoes and peppers and stir
to mix. Season again. Cover with the lid,
bring to the boil, then reduce the heat and
simmer gently for 45–55 minutes or until
the lamb is very tender. Stir occasionally
during cooking and add a little water if
the sauce becomes too dry. Meanwhile,
cook the pasta in a large pan of boiling
salted water, according to the packet
instructions, until tender or *al dente*.
Drain well. Remove and discard the bay
leaves from the lamb sauce before serving
it with the cooked pasta.

NUTRITIONAL NOTES
Per portion:

Energy	179Kcals/755kJ
Total fat	5g
Saturated fat	1.8g
Cholesterol	28mg
Fibre	1.4g

COOK'S TIP
You can make your own fresh
maccheroni alla chitarra or buy the
dried pasta from an Italian
delicatessen. Alternatively, this sauce
is just as good served with ordinary
spaghetti or long or short macaroni.

VARIATION
The peppers don't have to be red. Use
yellow, orange or green if you prefer;
either one colour or a mixture.

LASAGNE

This is a delicious low-fat version of the classic Italian lasagne, ideal served with a mixed salad
and crusty bread for an appetizing supper with friends.

INGREDIENTS

1 large onion, chopped
2 garlic cloves, crushed
500g/1¼lb extra-lean minced (ground)
beef or turkey
450g/1lb passata (bottled
strained tomatoes)
5ml/1 tsp dried mixed herbs
225g/8oz frozen leaf spinach, defrosted
200g/7oz lasagne verdi
200g/7oz low-fat cottage cheese

FOR THE SAUCE

25g/1oz low-fat spread
25g/1oz plain (all-purpose) flour
300ml/½ pint/1¼ cups skimmed milk
1.5ml/¼ tsp ground nutmeg
25g/1oz freshly grated Parmesan cheese
salt and ground black pepper

SERVES 8

1 Put the onion, garlic and minced meat
into a non-stick pan. Cook quickly for 5
minutes, stirring with a wooden spoon to
separate the pieces, until the meat is
lightly browned all over.

COOK'S TIP

Make sure you use the type of lasagne
that does not require any pre-cooking
for this recipe.

2 Add the passata, herbs and seasoning
and stir to mix. Bring to the boil, cover,
then reduce the heat and simmer for
about 30 minutes, stirring occasionally.

3 Make the sauce: put all the sauce
ingredients, except the Parmesan cheese,
into a pan. Cook until the sauce thickens,
whisking continuously until bubbling and
smooth. Turn the heat off. Adjust the
seasoning to taste, add the grated
Parmesan cheese to the sauce but not all
(set roughly a fifth aside) and stir to mix.

NUTRITIONAL NOTES
Per portion:

Energy	244Kcals/1032kJ
Total fat	4.8g
Saturated fat	1.9g
Cholesterol	37.9mg
Fibre	2g

4 Preheat the oven to 190°C/375°F/Gas 5.
Lay the spinach leaves out on sheets of
absorbent kitchen paper and pat them
until they are dry.

5 Layer the meat mixture, lasagne,
cottage cheese and spinach leaves in a
2 litre/3½ pint/8 cup ovenproof dish,
starting and ending with a layer of meat.

6 Spoon the sauce over the top to cover,
sprinkle with the remaining Parmesan,
and bake in the oven for 40–50 minutes
or until bubbling. Serve immediately.

FISH AND SHELLFISH

FISH *is naturally low in fat and pastas and risottos create a wonderful basis for many delicious and* NUTRITIOUS *low-fat* ITALIAN *fish and shellfish dishes. This section includes a* TEMPTING *selection of no-fuss recipes, using a variety of fish and* SHELLFISH, *to please every palate. Choose from Tagliatelle with* SCALLOPS, *Trout and Prosciutto risotto Rolls or* MONKFISH *with Tomato and Olive Sauce.*

ITALIAN FISH STEW

The different regions of Italy have their own variations of this low-fat dish. Buy some of the fish whole so you can simmer them, then remove the cooked flesh and strain the juices for the stock.

INGREDIENTS

900g/2lb mixture of fish fillets or steaks,
such as monkfish, cod, haddock, halibut
or hake
900g/2lb mixture of conger eel, red or grey
mullet, snapper or small white fish
1 onion, halved
1 celery stick, roughly chopped
225g/8oz squid
225g/8oz fresh mussels
675g/1¹/2lb ripe tomatoes
15ml/1 tbsp olive oil
1 large onion, thinly sliced
3 garlic cloves, crushed
5ml/1 tsp saffron threads
150ml/¹/4 pint/²/3 cup dry white wine
90ml/6 tbsp chopped fresh parsley
salt and ground black pepper
croûtons, to serve (optional)

SERVES 6

1 Remove and discard any skin and bones from the fish fillets or steaks, cut the fish into large pieces and reserve. Place the bones in a pan with all the remaining fish.

2 Add the onion and celery and cover with water. Bring almost to the boil, then reduce the heat and simmer for about 30 minutes. Lift out the fish and remove the flesh from the bones. Reserve the flesh and discard the bones. Strain and reserve the stock and discard the contents of the sieve.

3 To prepare the squid, twist the head and tentacles away from the body. Cut the head from the tentacles. Discard the body contents and peel the skin. Wash the tentacles and bodies and dry on kitchen paper. Scrub the mussels, discarding any that are damaged or open ones that do not close when tapped.

4 Plunge the tomatoes into a bowl of boiling water for 30 seconds, then refresh in cold water. Peel away and discard the skins and chop the tomatoes roughly.

5 Heat the oil in a large pan or sauté pan. Add the onion and garlic and fry gently for 3 minutes. Add the squid and the reserved uncooked white fish, and fry quickly on all sides, stirring frequently. Remove from the pan, and drain.

6 Add 475ml/16fl oz/2 cups reserved fish stock, the tomatoes and saffron to the pan. Pour in the wine. Bring to the boil, then reduce the heat and simmer for about 5 minutes. Add the mussels, cover, and cook for 3–4 minutes until the mussels have opened. Discard any that remain closed. Season the sauce and add all the fish. Cook gently for 5 minutes until hot, stirring occasionally. Sprinkle with the parsley and serve with croûtons, if using.

NUTRITIONAL NOTES
Per portion:

Energy	321Kcals/1355kJ
Total fat	5g
Saturated fat	0.7g
Cholesterol	136.8mg
Fibre	1g

MONKFISH WITH TOMATO AND OLIVE SAUCE

—

This low-fat Italian dish comes from the coast of Calabria in southern Italy. Serve with garlic-flavoured mashed potatoes for an ideal family meal.

INGREDIENTS

450g/1lb fresh mussels in their
shells, scrubbed
a few fresh basil sprigs
2 garlic cloves, roughly chopped
300ml/1/2 pint/1 1/4 cups dry white wine
15ml/1 tbsp olive oil
900g/2lb monkfish fillets, skinned and cut
into large chunks
1 onion, finely chopped
500g/1 1/4lb jar sugocasa or passata
(bottled strained tomatoes)
15ml/1 tbsp sun-dried tomato purée (paste)
50g/2oz/1/2 cup pitted black olives
salt and ground black pepper
extra fresh basil leaves, to garnish

SERVES 4

1 Put the mussels in a flameproof casserole with some of the basil leaves, the garlic and the wine. Cover and bring to the boil. Lower the heat and simmer for 5 minutes, shaking the pan frequently. Remove the mussels, discarding any that fail to open. Strain and reserve the cooking liquid.

2 Heat the oil in a flameproof casserole, add the monkfish pieces and sauté over a medium heat until they just change colour. Remove the fish from the pan, place on a plate and set aside.

3 Add the onion to the juices in the casserole and cook gently for about 5 minutes, stirring frequently, until softened. Add the sugocasa or passata, the reserved cooking liquid from the mussels and the tomato purée. Season to taste with salt and pepper. Bring to the boil, stirring, then reduce the heat, cover and allow to simmer for 20 minutes, stirring occasionally.

NUTRITIONAL NOTES
Per portion:

Energy	221Kcals/931kJ
Total fat	4.6g
Saturated fat	0.7g
Cholesterol	81.9mg
Fibre	1.1g

4 Pull off and discard the top shells from the cooked mussels and set them aside. Add the monkfish pieces to the tomato sauce and cook gently for 5 minutes. Gently stir in the olives and remaining basil, then adjust the seasoning. Place the mussels in their half-shells on top of the sauce, cover the pan and heat the mussels through for 1–2 minutes. Serve immediately, garnished with basil leaves.

PRAWNS IN FRESH TOMATO SAUCE
—

**Fresh prawns are cooked and served in a fresh tomato sauce to create this appetizing
Italian-style low-fat dish.**

INGREDIENTS
20ml/4 tsp olive oil
1 onion, finely chopped
1 celery stick, finely chopped
*1 small red (bell) pepper, deseeded
and chopped*
120ml/4fl oz/¹/2 cup red wine
15ml/1 tbsp wine vinegar
*400g/14oz can plum tomatoes, chopped,
with their juice*
*1kg/2¹/4lb uncooked prawns (shrimp),
in their shells*
2–3 garlic cloves, finely chopped
*45ml/3 tbsp finely chopped
fresh parsley*
*1 dried chilli, crumbled or
chopped (optional)*
salt and ground black pepper

SERVES 6

NUTRITIONAL NOTES
Per portion:

Energy	114Kcals/476kJ
Total fat	3.2g
Saturated fat	0.6g
Cholesterol	49.2mg
Fibre	0.8g

1 Heat half the oil in a heavy pan. Add
the onion and cook over a low heat until
soft, stirring occasionally. Stir in the
chopped celery and pepper and cook for
5 minutes. Increase the heat and add the
wine, vinegar and tomatoes. Bring the
mixture to the boil and cook for
5 minutes, stirring occasionally. Reduce
the heat, cover the pan and simmer for
about 30 minutes, until the vegetables
are soft, stirring occasionally.

2 Remove the pan from the heat and
allow the vegetable mixture to cool a
little, then purée through a food mill to
make a tomato sauce. Set aside.

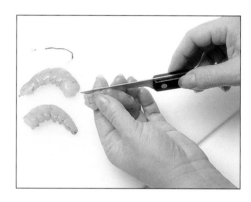

3 Shell the prawns. Make a shallow
incision with a small, sharp knife along
the back of each prawn and remove the
long, black vein. Set the prawns aside.

4 Heat the remaining oil in a clean,
heavy pan. Stir in the garlic and parsley,
plus the chilli, if using. Cook over a
medium heat, stirring, until the garlic is
golden. Stir in the prepared tomato sauce
and bring to the boil.

5 Stir in the prepared prawns. Bring the
sauce back to the boil. Reduce the heat
slightly and simmer, stirring occasionally,
until the prawns are pink and stiff: this
will take about 6–8 minutes, depending
on their size. Season to taste and serve.

MEDITERRANEAN FISH CUTLETS

These low-fat fish cutlets are ideal served with boiled potatoes, broccoli and carrots for
a delicious Italian supper.

2 Meanwhile, place the fish in a frying
pan, pour over the stock and/or wine and
add the bay leaf, peppercorns and lemon
rind. Cover and simmer for 10 minutes or
until the fish is cooked and the flesh
flakes easily.

3 Using a slotted spoon, transfer the fish
to a heated serving dish. Strain the fish
stock into the tomato sauce and boil to
reduce slightly. Season the sauce, pour it
over the fish and serve immediately,
sprinkled with the chopped fresh parsley
to garnish.

INGREDIENTS

4 white fish cutlets, about 150g/5oz each
about 150ml/¹/4 pint/²/3 cup fish stock or
dry white wine (or a mixture of the two),
for poaching
1 bay leaf, a few black peppercorns and a
strip of pared lemon rind, for flavouring
chopped fresh parsley, to garnish

FOR THE TOMATO SAUCE

400g/14oz can chopped tomatoes
1 garlic clove, crushed
*15ml/1 tbsp pastis or other aniseed-(anise
seed-) flavoured liqueur*
15ml/1 tbsp drained capers
12–16 pitted black olives
salt and ground black pepper

SERVES 4

1 To make the tomato sauce, place the
chopped tomatoes, garlic, pastis or other
liqueur, capers and olives in a pan.
Season to taste with salt and pepper and
cook over a low heat for about 15 minutes,
stirring occasionally.

COOK'S TIP

Remove the skin from the fish cutlets
and use fewer olives to reduce calories
and fat even further. Use 450g/1lb
fresh tomatoes, skinned and chopped,
in place of canned.

NUTRITIONAL NOTES

Per portion:

Energy	165Kcals/685kJ
Total fat	3.55g
Saturated fat	0.5g
Cholesterol	69mg
Fibre	0.8g

MONKFISH WITH PEPPERED CITRUS MARINADE

—

A fresh citrus fruit marinade adds delicious flavour to monkfish fillets and creates a low-fat, appetizing dish ideal for cooking and eating *al fresco*.

INGREDIENTS

2 monkfish tails, about 350g/12oz each
1 lime
1 lemon
2 oranges
a handful of fresh thyme sprigs
20ml/4 tsp olive oil
15ml/1 tbsp mixed peppercorns,
roughly crushed
salt and ground black pepper

SERVES 4

1 Remove and discard any skin from the monkfish tails.

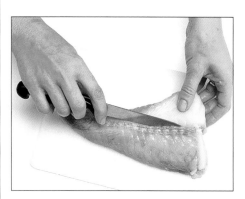

2 Cut carefully down one side of the backbone, sliding the knife between the bone and flesh, to remove the fillet on one side. (You can ask your fishmonger to do this for you.)

NUTRITIONAL NOTES
Per portion:

Energy	176Kcals/741kJ
Total fat	5g
Saturated fat	0.7g
Cholesterol	80.6mg
Fibre	0g

3 Turn the fish and repeat on the other side. Repeat on the second tail. Discard the bones. Lay the fillets out flat.

4 Cut two slices from each of the citrus fruits and arrange over two fillets. Add a few sprigs of thyme and season. Finely grate the rind from the remaining fruit and sprinkle over the fish.

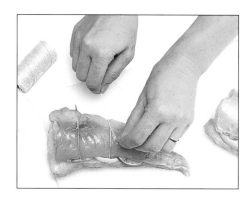

5 Lay the other two fillets on top and tie them firmly at intervals, with fine cotton string, to hold them in shape. Place in a wide, shallow, non-metallic dish.

6 Squeeze the juice from the citrus fruits and mix it with the oil and more salt and black pepper.

7 Spoon the juice mixture over the fish. Cover and leave to marinate for about an hour, turning occasionally and spooning the marinade over it.

8 Drain the monkfish, reserving the marinade, and sprinkle with the crushed peppercorns. Cook on a medium hot barbecue for 15–20 minutes, basting the fish with the marinade and turning it occasionally, until it is evenly cooked. Serve immediately.

VARIATION
You can also use this marinade for monkfish kebabs.

ITALIAN FISH PARCELS
—

Fresh sea bass fillets are topped with mixed Italian vegetables, then cooked on a barbecue or in
the oven to create this tasty dish, ideal for eating *al fresco*.

INGREDIENTS

4 pieces skinless sea bass fillet or 4 whole
small sea bass
10ml/2 tsp olive oil for brushing
2 shallots, thinly sliced
1 garlic clove, chopped
15ml/1 tbsp capers
6 sun-dried tomatoes, finely chopped
4 black olives, pitted and thinly sliced
finely grated rind and juice of 1 lemon
5ml/1 tsp paprika
salt and ground black pepper

SERVES 4

1 If you are using whole fish, gut them,
taking care not to insert the knife too far.
Use a teaspoon or your fingers to scrape
out the contents. Leave the scales on as
they will hold the fragile fish together
during cooking.

2 Wash the cavity and the outside of the
fish thoroughly with cold water.

3 Cut four large squares of double-
thickness foil, large enough to enclose
the fish. Brush each square with a little
olive oil.

4 Place a piece of fish in the centre of
each piece of foil and season well with
salt and pepper.

5 Cover with the shallots, garlic, capers,
sun-dried tomatoes, olives and grated
lemon rind. Sprinkle with the lemon juice
and paprika.

6 Fold the foil over to enclose the fish
loosely, sealing the edges firmly so that
none of the juices can escape.

7 Place on a moderately hot barbecue
and cook for 8–10 minutes. Then open
up the tops of the parcels and serve.

COOK'S TIPS

• When choosing fish, look for bright,
slightly bulging eyes and shiny, faintly
slimy skin. Open up the gills to check
that they are clear red or dark pink
and prod the fish lightly to check
that the flesh is springy. All fish
should have only a faint, pleasant
smell; you can tell a stale fish a mile
off by its disagreeable odour.

• Sea bass are prized for their delicate
white flesh, and these slim, elegant fish
are almost always sold whole. They
don't have any irritating small bones,
and as a result are never cheap.

NUTRITIONAL NOTES
Per portion:

Energy	117Kcals/492kJ
Total fat	4.5g
Saturated fat	0.6g
Cholesterol	50.2mg
Fibre	0.1g

VARIATIONS

• These parcels can also be baked
in the oven: place them on a baking
sheet and cook at 200°C/400°F/Gas 6
for 15–20 minutes.

• Sea bass is good for this recipe, but
you could also use small whole trout,
or white fish fillet such as cod
or haddock.

BAKED FISH WITH ITALIAN VEGETABLE SAUCE

—

Fresh plaice or flounder fillets are oven-baked in an Italian mixed vegetable sauce to create a very low-fat meal for family or friends.

INGREDIENTS

4 large plaice or flounder fillets
2 small red onions
120ml/4fl oz/1/2 cup vegetable stock
60ml/4 tbsp dry red wine
1 garlic clove, crushed
2 courgettes (zucchini), sliced
1 yellow (bell) pepper, deseeded and sliced
400g/14oz can chopped tomatoes
15ml/1 tbsp chopped fresh thyme
salt and ground black pepper
fresh thyme sprigs, to garnish
potato gratin, to serve

SERVES 4

2 Cut each onion into eight wedges. Put into a heavy pan with the vegetable stock. Cover, bring to the boil and simmer for 5 minutes. Uncover and continue to cook, stirring occasionally, until the stock has reduced entirely. Add the red wine and crushed garlic to the pan and continue to cook until the onions are soft, stirring occasionally.

3 Stir in the courgettes, yellow pepper, tomatoes and chopped thyme and season to taste. Simmer for 3 minutes. Spoon the sauce into a large casserole.

4 Fold each fillet in half and put on top of the vegetable sauce. Cover and cook in the oven for 15–20 minutes, until the fish is opaque and flakes easily. Garnish with fresh thyme sprigs and serve with a potato gratin.

COOK'S TIP
Skinless white fish fillets such as plaice or flounder are low in fat and make an ideal tasty and nutritious basis for many low-fat recipes like this.

1 Preheat the oven to 180°C/350°F/Gas 4. Lay the fillets skin-side down and, holding the tail end, push a sharp knife between the skin and flesh in a sawing movement. Hold the knife at a slight angle with the blade towards the skin. Discard the skin and set the fish aside.

NUTRITIONAL NOTES
Per portion:

Energy	144Kcals/612kJ
Total fat	2.7g
Saturated fat	0.4g
Cholesterol	46.2mg
Fibre	1.5g

BAKED COD WITH TOMATOES

For the very best flavour, use firm sun-ripened tomatoes for this Italian tomato sauce and make sure it is fairly thick before spooning it over the cod. Serve with boiled new potatoes and a salad.

2 Bring the sauce just to the boil, then reduce the heat slightly and cook, uncovered, for 15–20 minutes until thick, stirring occasionally. Stir in the parsley.

3 Lightly grease an ovenproof dish, put in the cod cutlets and spoon an equal quantity of the tomato sauce on to each. Sprinkle the breadcrumbs over the top.

4 Bake in the oven for 20–30 minutes, basting occasionally with the sauce, until the fish is cooked through, and the breadcrumbs are golden. Serve hot with new potatoes and a mixed green salad.

INGREDIENTS

10ml/2 tsp olive oil
1 onion, chopped
2 garlic cloves, finely chopped
450g/1lb tomatoes, peeled, deseeded and chopped
5ml/1 tsp tomato purée (paste)
60ml/4 tbsp dry white wine
60ml/4 tbsp chopped fresh flat leaf parsley
4 cod cutlets
30ml/2 tbsp dried breadcrumbs
salt and ground black pepper
boiled new potatoes and mixed green salad, to serve

SERVES 4

1 Preheat the oven to 190ºC/375ºF/Gas 5. Heat the oil in a frying pan and fry the onion for about 5 minutes, stirring occasionally. Add the garlic, tomatoes, tomato purée, wine and seasoning and stir to mix.

COOK'S TIP

For extra speed, use a 400g/14oz can of chopped tomatoes in place of the fresh tomatoes and 5–10ml/1–2 tsp ready-crushed garlic in place of the garlic cloves.

NUTRITIONAL NOTES

Per portion:

Energy	151Kcals/647kJ
Total fat	1.5g
Saturated fat	0.2g
Cholesterol	55.2mg
Fibre	2.42g

TROUT AND PROSCIUTTO RISOTTO ROLLS

This makes a delicious and elegant low-fat meal. The risotto – made with porcini or chanterelle mushrooms and prawns – is an ideal accompaniment for the flavourful trout rolls.

INGREDIENTS

10ml/2 tsp olive oil
8 large raw prawns (shrimp),
peeled and deveined
1 onion, chopped
225g/8oz/generous 1 cup risotto rice
about 105ml/7 tbsp white wine
about 750ml/1¼ pints/3 cups simmering
fish or chicken stock
15g/½oz/2 tbsp dried porcini or
chanterelle mushrooms, soaked for
10 minutes in warm water to cover
4 trout fillets, skinned
4 thin slices of prosciutto
salt and freshly ground black pepper
capers, to garnish

SERVES 4

2 Add the onion to the oil in the pan. Fry over a low heat for 3–4 minutes until soft, stirring occasionally. Add the rice and stir for 3–4 minutes until the grains are evenly coated in oil. Add 75ml/5 tbsp of the wine and then the stock, a little at a time, stirring over a gentle heat and allowing the rice to absorb the liquid before adding more.

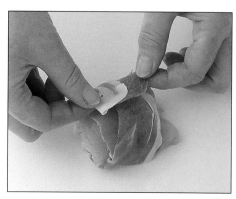

5 Take a trout fillet, place a spoonful of risotto at one end and roll up. Wrap each fillet in a slice of prosciutto and place in a lightly greased ovenproof dish.

6 Spoon any remaining risotto around the fish fillets and sprinkle over the rest of the wine. Bake the rolls in the oven for 15–20 minutes until the fish is cooked and tender. Spoon the risotto on to a platter, top with the trout rolls and garnish with some fat capers. Serve at once.

1 First make the risotto. Heat the oil in a heavy pan or deep frying pan and fry the prawns very briefly until flecked with pink, stirring. Lift out using a slotted spoon and transfer to a plate. Set aside.

3 Drain the mushrooms, reserving the liquid, and cut the larger ones in half. Towards the end of cooking, stir the mushrooms into the risotto with 15ml/ 1 tbsp of the reserved mushroom liquid. If the rice is not yet *al dente*, add a little more stock or mushroom liquid and cook for 2–3 minutes more. Season to taste with salt and pepper.

4 Remove the pan from the heat and stir in the prawns. Preheat the oven to 190°C/ 375°F/Gas 5.

COOK'S TIP

Make sure you use proper risotto rice, such as arborio or carnaroli, for this recipe. Short grain rice will not give the right consistency.

NUTRITIONAL NOTES
Per portion:

Energy	245Kcals/1035kJ
Total fat	5g
Saturated fat	1.1g
Cholesterol	63.8mg
Fibre	0.3g

FARFALLE WITH TUNA

—

This is a quick and simple dish that makes a good low-fat weekday supper if you have canned
tomatoes and tuna in the pantry. Serve with crusty fresh Italian bread.

4 Meanwhile, cook the pasta in a large
pan of boiling salted water according to
the packet instructions, until tender or
al dente.

5 Drain the tuna and flake it with a fork.
Add to the sauce with about 60ml/4 tbsp
of the pasta water and stir to mix. Adjust
the seasoning to taste.

6 Drain the pasta well and tip it into a
warmed serving bowl. Pour the sauce
over the top and toss to mix. Serve
immediately, garnished with oregano.

INGREDIENTS

15ml/1 tbsp olive oil
1 small onion, finely chopped
1 garlic clove, finely chopped
400g/14oz can chopped Italian
plum tomatoes
45ml/3 tbsp dry white wine
8–10 pitted black olives, sliced into rings
10ml/2 tsp chopped fresh oregano or
5ml/1 tsp dried oregano, plus extra fresh
oregano, to garnish
350g/12oz/3 cups dried farfalle
175g/6oz can tuna in brine
salt and freshly ground black pepper

SERVES 4

1 Heat the olive oil in a medium
frying pan, and add the chopped onion
and garlic.

2 Cook the onion and garlic gently for
2–3 minutes until the onion is soft and
golden, stirring occasionally.

3 Add the tomatoes and bring to the boil,
then add the white wine and simmer for a
minute or so. Stir in the olives and
oregano, with salt and pepper to taste,
then cover and cook for 20–25 minutes,
stirring occasionally.

NUTRITIONAL NOTES

Per portion:

Energy	387Kcals/1643kJ
Total fat	4.9g
Saturated fat	0.8g
Cholesterol	21.3mg
Fibre	3.5g

VERMICELLI WITH CLAM SAUCE

This recipe originates from the city of Naples, where both fresh tomato sauce and shellfish
are traditionally served with vermicelli. The two are combined for a tasty, low-fat dish.

INGREDIENTS

1kg/2¼lb fresh clams
250ml/8fl oz/1 cup dry white wine
2 garlic cloves, bruised
1 large handful of fresh flat leaf parsley
10ml/2 tsp olive oil
1 small onion, finely chopped
8 ripe Italian plum tomatoes, peeled,
deseeded and finely chopped
½–1 fresh red chilli, deseeded and
finely chopped
350g/12oz dried vermicelli
salt and ground black pepper

SERVES 4

1 Scrub the clams thoroughly under cold running water and discard any that are open or that do not close when sharply tapped against the work surface.

2 Pour the white wine into a large pan, add the bruised garlic cloves and half the parsley, then add the clams. Cover tightly with the lid and bring to the boil over a high heat. Cook for about 5 minutes, shaking the pan frequently, until the clams have opened.

3 Tip the clams into a large colander set over a bowl and let the liquid drain through. Leave the clams until cool enough to handle, then remove about two-thirds of them from their shells, tipping the clam liquor into the bowl of cooking liquid.

4 Discard any clams that have failed to open. Set both shelled and unshelled clams aside, keeping the unshelled clams warm in a bowl covered with a lid. Reserve the cooking liquid and set aside.

5 Heat the oil in a pan, add the onion and cook gently, stirring frequently, for about 5 minutes until softened. Add the tomatoes, then the clam liquid. Add the chilli, season to taste, and stir.

6 Bring to the boil, half cover, then simmer gently for 15–20 minutes, stirring occasionally. Meanwhile, cook the pasta in a large pan of boiling salted water, according to the packet instructions. Chop the remaining parsley finely.

NUTRITIONAL NOTES

Per portion:

Energy	536Kcals/2262kJ
Total fat	4.7g
Saturated fat	0.4g
Cholesterol	0mg
Fibre	2.4g

7 Add the shelled clams to the sauce, stir well and heat through very gently for 2–3 minutes, stirring occasionally.

8 Drain the cooked pasta well and tip it into a warmed bowl. Taste the clam and tomato sauce and adjust the seasoning, then pour the sauce over the pasta and toss everything together well. Garnish with the reserved clams in their shells, sprinkle the chopped parsley over the pasta and serve immediately.

TAGLIATELLE WITH SCALLOPS

—

Scallops and brandy add a taste of luxury to this appetizing pasta sauce, ideal as a supper dish.

INGREDIENTS
200g/7oz scallops, sliced
30ml/2 tbsp plain (all-purpose) flour
15ml/1 tbsp olive oil
2 spring onions (scallions), cut into thin rings
1/2–1 small fresh red chilli, deseeded and very finely chopped
30ml/2 tbsp finely chopped fresh flat leaf parsley
60ml/4 tbsp brandy
105ml/7 tbsp fish stock
275g/10oz fresh spinach-flavoured tagliatelle
salt and freshly ground black pepper

SERVES 4

1 Toss the scallops in the flour, shaking the excess. Bring a large pan of salted water to the boil for the pasta. Meanwhile, heat the oil in a frying pan. Add the spring onions, chilli and half the parsley and cook, stirring frequently, for 1–2 minutes over a medium heat. Add the scallops and toss for 1–2 minutes.

2 Pour the brandy over the scallops, then set it alight. When the flames have died down, pour in the stock, season and stir. Simmer for 2–3 minutes, then cover and remove from the heat. Cook the pasta according to the packet instructions. Drain, add to the sauce and toss over a medium heat until well mixed. Serve immediately.

NUTRITIONAL NOTES
Per portion:

Energy	372Kcals/1576kJ
Total fat	4.8g
Saturated fat	0.7g
Cholesterol	0.0mg
Fibre	2.2g

SPAGHETTI WITH SQUID AND PEAS

—

In Tuscany, squid is often cooked with peas in a tomato sauce. This low-fat recipe is a tasty variation on the theme that works very well.

INGREDIENTS
450g/1lb prepared squid
10ml/2 tsp olive oil
1 small onion, finely chopped
400g/14oz can chopped Italian plum tomatoes
1 garlic clove, finely chopped
15ml/1 tbsp red wine vinegar
5ml/1 tsp sugar
10ml/2 tsp finely chopped fresh rosemary
115g/4oz/1 cup frozen peas
275g/10oz dried spaghetti
15ml/1 tbsp chopped fresh flat leaf parsley
salt and ground black pepper

SERVES 4

1 Cut the prepared squid into strips about 5mm/1/4in wide. Finely chop any tentacles. Set aside. Heat the oil in a frying pan, add the onion and cook gently, stirring, for about 5 minutes until softened. Add the squid, tomatoes, garlic, vinegar and sugar and stir to mix.

NUTRITIONAL NOTES
Per portion:

Energy	285Kcals/1206kJ
Total fat	4g
Saturated fat	0.4g
Cholesterol	0.0mg
Fibre	3g

2 Add the rosemary and seasoning. Bring to the boil, stirring, then cover, reduce the heat, and simmer for 20 minutes, stirring occasionally. Stir in the peas and cook for a further 10 minutes. Cook the pasta according to the packet instructions. Serve with the sauce and the parsley.

VEGETARIAN
DISHES
AND
VEGETABLES

VEGETARIAN *dishes and vegetables*
play an important part in a LOW-FAT
diet, providing nutritious and filling recipes
made from FRESH INGREDIENTS
that all the family will enjoy. Many of the
dishes are SIMPLE *but substantial and*
provide an enticing menu, including Baked
CHEESE POLENTA *with Tomato Sauce,*
Fennel Gratin, Roasted Mediterranean
Vegetables and CAPONATA.

CAPONATA

—

This dish is a quintessential part of Sicilian antipasti and is a rich, spicy mixture of aubergine, tomatoes, capers and celery. Serve with warm crusty bread and olives.

3 Cover the surface of the vegetables with a circle of waxed paper and simmer for 8–10 minutes. Remove and discard the paper.

4 Add the capers and olives to the pan, then season to taste with salt and mix together well.

5 Spoon the caponata into a bowl, garnish with chopped fresh parsley and serve at room temperature.

INGREDIENTS

20ml/4 tsp olive oil
1 large onion, sliced
2 celery sticks, sliced
450g/1lb aubergines (eggplant), diced
5 ripe tomatoes, chopped
1 garlic clove, crushed
45ml/3 tbsp red wine vinegar
15ml/1 tbsp sugar
30ml/2 tbsp capers
12 olives
pinch of salt
60ml/4 tbsp chopped fresh parsley, to garnish

SERVES 4

1 Heat half the oil in a large heavy pan. Add the onion and celery and cook over a gentle heat for 3–4 minutes to soften, stirring occasionally.

2 Add the remainder of the oil with the aubergines and stir to mix. Cook until the aubergines begin to colour, stirring occasionally, then stir in the tomatoes, garlic, vinegar and sugar.

NUTRITIONAL NOTES
Per portion:

Energy	81Kcals/340kJ
Total fat	4.7g
Saturated fat	0.7g
Cholesterol	0mg
Fibre	2.9g

KOHLRABI STUFFED WITH PEPPERS

The slightly sharp flavour of the peppers is an excellent foil to the more earthy flavour of the kohlrabi in this delicious low-fat Italian-style vegetable dish.

INGREDIENTS

4 small kohlrabis, about
175–225g/6–8oz each
about 400ml/14fl oz/1²/₃ cups hot
vegetable stock
1 small red (bell) pepper
1 small green (bell) pepper
15ml/1 tbsp sunflower oil
1 onion, chopped
salt and ground black pepper
fresh flat leaf parsley, to garnish (optional)

SERVES 4

1 Preheat the oven to 180°C/350°F/Gas 4. Trim the kohlrabis and arrange in an ovenproof dish.

2 Pour over enough stock to come about halfway up the vegetables. Cover and braise in the oven for about 30 minutes, until tender. Transfer to a plate and allow to cool, reserving the stock.

3 Deseed and slice the peppers. Heat the oil in a frying pan and fry the onion over a gentle heat for 3–4 minutes, stirring occasionally. Add the peppers and cook for a further 2–3 minutes, until the onion is lightly browned, stirring occasionally.

4 Add the reserved vegetable stock and a little seasoning and allow to simmer, uncovered, over a moderate heat, until the stock has almost all evaporated, stirring occasionally.

5 Scoop out the insides of the kohlrabis and chop roughly. Stir into the onion and pepper mixture and adjust the seasoning to taste. Arrange the kohlrabi shells in a shallow ovenproof dish.

6 Spoon the pepper filling into the kohlrabi shells. Place in the oven for 5–10 minutes to heat through and then serve, garnished with a sprig of flat leaf parsley, if you like.

NUTRITIONAL NOTES
Per portion:

Energy	112Kcals/470kJ
Total fat	4.63g
Saturated fat	0.55g
Cholesterol	0mg
Fibre	5.8g

COURGETTES WITH ONION AND GARLIC

Use good-quality olive oil and sunflower oil for this dish. The olive oil gives the dish a delicious fragrance without overpowering the courgettes, making this an ideal vegetable accompaniment.

INGREDIENTS

10ml/2 tsp olive oil
10ml/2 tsp sunflower oil
1 large onion, chopped
1 garlic clove, crushed
4–5 courgettes (zucchini), cut into
1cm/¹/₂in slices
150ml/¹/₄ pint/²/₃ cup vegetable stock
2.5ml/¹/₂ tsp chopped fresh oregano
salt and ground black pepper
chopped fresh parsley, to garnish

SERVES 4

1 Heat the olive and sunflower oils in a large frying pan and fry the onion with the garlic over a moderate heat for 5–6 minutes, stirring occasionally, until the onion has softened and is beginning to brown.

2 Add the sliced courgettes and fry for about 4 minutes until they begin to be flecked with brown, stirring frequently.

3 Stir in the stock, oregano and seasoning and simmer gently for 8–10 minutes or until the liquid has almost evaporated, stirring occasionally.

4 Spoon the courgettes into a warmed serving dish, sprinkle with chopped parsley and serve.

NUTRITIONAL NOTES
Per portion:

Energy	47Kcals/192kJ
Total fat	4.1g
Saturated fat	0.5g
Cholesterol	0mg
Fibre	0.5g

COURGETTES IN CITRUS SAUCE
—

These tender baby courgettes served in a virtually fat-free citrus sauce make this a tasty and low-fat accompaniment to grilled fish fillets.

INGREDIENTS

350g/12oz baby courgettes (zucchini)
4 spring onions (scallions), thinly sliced
2.5cm/1in piece of fresh root ginger, peeled and grated
30ml/2 tbsp white wine vinegar
15ml/1 tbsp light soy sauce
5ml/1 tsp soft light brown sugar
45ml/3 tbsp vegetable stock
finely grated rind and juice of 1/2 lemon and 1/2 orange
5ml/1 tsp cornflour (cornstarch)

SERVES 4

1 Place the courgettes in a pan of lightly salted boiling water and cook for 3–4 minutes, or until just tender. Drain well and return to the pan. Set aside.

2 Meanwhile, put all the remaining ingredients, except the cornflour, into a pan and bring to the boil, stirring occasionally. Simmer for 3 minutes.

3 Blend the cornflour with 10ml/2 tsp cold water in a small bowl and stir into the sauce. Bring the sauce to the boil, stirring continuously, until the sauce has thickened.

4 Pour the sauce over the courgettes in the pan and heat gently, shaking the pan to coat them evenly. Transfer to a warmed serving dish and serve.

COOK'S TIP
If baby courgettes are unavailable, you can use larger ones, but they should be cooked whole so that they don't absorb too much water. After cooking, halve them lengthways and cut them into 10cm/4in lengths.

NUTRITIONAL NOTES
Per portion:

Energy	33Kcals/138kJ
Total fat	2.18g
Saturated fat	0.42g
Cholesterol	0.09mg
Fibre	0.92g

FENNEL GRATIN

This is one of the best ways to eat fresh fennel as a snack or vegetable accompaniment.

INGREDIENTS
2 fennel bulbs, about 675g/1¹/2lb total
300ml/¹/2 pint/1¹/4 cups semi-
skimmed (low-fat) milk
15g/¹/2oz/1 tbsp butter
15ml/1 tbsp plain (all-purpose) flour
25g/1oz/scant ¹/2 cup dry
white breadcrumbs
40g/1¹/2oz Gruyère cheese, grated
salt and ground black pepper

SERVES 6

1 Preheat the oven to 240°C/475°F/Gas 9. Discard the stalks and root ends from the fennel. Slice the fennel into quarters and place in a large pan. Pour over the milk, bring to the boil, then simmer for 10–15 minutes until tender.

2 Grease a small baking dish. Remove the fennel pieces with a slotted spoon, reserving the milk. Arrange the fennel pieces in the dish.

3 Melt the butter in a small pan and add the flour. Stir well, then gradually whisk in the reserved milk. Cook the sauce until thickened, stirring.

4 Pour the sauce over the fennel pieces, sprinkle with the breadcrumbs and Gruyère. Season and bake in the oven for about 20 minutes until browned. Serve.

VARIATION
Instead of Gruyère, any strong cheese such as Parmesan, Pecorino, mature (sharp) Cheddar works just as well.

NUTRITIONAL NOTES
Per portion:

Energy	89Kcals/371kJ
Total fat	4.8g
Saturated fat	2.9g
Cholesterol	8.24mg
Fibre	2.5g

ITALIAN SWEET-AND-SOUR ONIONS

Onions are naturally sweet, and when they are cooked at a high temperature the sweetness intensifies. Serve these delicious onions with cooked lean meat or cooked fresh vegetables.

INGREDIENTS
25g/1oz/2 tbsp butter
75ml/5 tbsp sugar
120ml/4fl oz/¹/2 cup white wine vinegar
30ml/2 tbsp balsamic vinegar
675g/1¹/2lb pickling (pearl) onions, peeled
salt and ground black pepper

SERVES 6

COOK'S TIP
This recipe also looks delicious when made with either yellow or red onions, cut into slices. Cooking times vary, depending on the size of the pieces.

1 Melt the butter in a large pan over a gentle heat. Add the sugar and cook until it begins to dissolve, stirring constantly.

2 Add the vinegars to the pan with the onions and heat gently. Season, cover and cook over a moderate heat for 20–25 minutes, stirring occasionally, until the onions are soft when pierced with a knife. Serve hot.

NUTRITIONAL NOTES
Per portion:

Energy	106Kcals/447kJ
Total fat	3.6g
Saturated fat	2.2g
Cholesterol	9.5mg
Fibre	1.3g

ROASTED MEDITERRANEAN VEGETABLES

Mixed Mediterranean vegetables are oven-roasted in olive oil with garlic and rosemary in this really colourful and appetizing low-fat dish. The flavour is also wonderfully intense.

INGREDIENTS

1 red (bell) pepper
1 yellow (bell) pepper
2 Spanish onions
2 large courgettes (zucchini)
1 large aubergine (eggplant) or 4 baby aubergines, trimmed
1 fennel bulb, thickly sliced
2 beefsteak tomatoes
8 fat garlic cloves
25ml/1½ tbsp olive oil
fresh rosemary sprigs
freshly ground black pepper
lemon wedges and black olives, to garnish (optional)

SERVES 6

3 Preheat the oven to 220°C/425°F/Gas 7. Spread the peppers, onions, courgettes, aubergines and fennel in a lightly greased shallow ovenproof dish or roasting pan or, if you like, arrange in rows to make a colourful design.

4 Cut each tomato in half and place, cut-side up, with the vegetables.

5 Tuck the garlic cloves in among the vegetables, then brush all the vegetables with the olive oil. Place some sprigs of rosemary among the vegetables and grind over some black pepper, particularly on the tomatoes.

6 Roast in the oven for 20–25 minutes, turning the vegetables halfway through the cooking time. Serve from the dish or on a flat platter, garnished with lemon wedges. Sprinkle a few black olives over the top just before serving, if you like.

NUTRITIONAL NOTES
Per portion:

Energy	72Kcals/299kJ
Total fat	4g
Saturated fat	0.6g
Cholesterol	0mg
Fibre	2.3g

1 Halve and seed the peppers, then cut them into large chunks. Peel the onions and cut into thick wedges.

2 Cut the courgettes and aubergine(s) into large chunks.

PEPPER GRATIN

Serve this simple but delicious Italian dish as a low-fat appetizer or snack with a small mixed
leaf salad and some good crusty bread to mop up the juices from the peppers.

3 Use a little of the olive oil to grease a
small baking dish. Arrange the pepper
strips in the dish.

4 Sprinkle the garlic, capers, olives and
chopped herbs on top. Season with salt
and pepper. Sprinkle over the fresh white
breadcrumbs and drizzle with the
remaining olive oil. Bake in the oven for
about 20 minutes until the breadcrumbs
have browned. Garnish with fresh herbs
and serve immediately.

INGREDIENTS

2 red (bell) peppers
15ml/1 tbsp extra virgin olive oil
1 garlic clove, finely chopped
5ml/1 tsp drained bottled capers
8 pitted black olives, roughly chopped
15ml/1 tbsp chopped fresh oregano
15ml/1 tbsp chopped fresh flat leaf parsley
60ml/4 tbsp fresh white breadcrumbs
salt and ground black pepper
fresh herbs, to garnish

SERVES 4

1 Preheat the oven to 200°C/400°F/Gas 6.
Place the peppers on a rack, cook under a
hot grill (broiler), turning occasionally
until they are blackened and blistered all
over. Remove from the heat and place in a
plastic bag. Seal and leave to cool.

2 When cool, peel the peppers. (Don't
skin them under the tap as the water
would wash away some of the delicious
smoky flavour.) Halve and remove and
discard the seeds, then cut the flesh into
large strips.

NUTRITIONAL NOTES
Per portion:

Energy	72Kcals/303kJ
Total fat	3.4g
Saturated fat	0.5g
Cholesterol	0mg
Fibre	0.9g

STUFFED AUBERGINES

This typical dish from the Ligurian region of Italy is spiked with paprika and allspice, a legacy from the days when spices from the East came into northern Italy via the port of Genoa.

INGREDIENTS

2 aubergines (eggplant), about 225g/8oz
each, stalks removed
275g/10oz potatoes, peeled and diced
15ml/1 tbsp olive oil
1 small onion, finely chopped
1 garlic clove, finely chopped
good pinch of ground allspice and paprika
30ml/2 tbsp skimmed milk
25g/1oz freshly grated Parmesan cheese
15ml/1 tbsp fresh white breadcrumbs
salt and ground black pepper
fresh mint sprigs, to garnish
salad leaves, to serve

SERVES 6

1 Bring a large pan of lightly salted water to the boil. Add the whole aubergines and cook for 5 minutes, turning frequently. Remove with a slotted spoon and set aside. Add the diced potatoes to the pan and boil for about 15 minutes or until cooked.

2 Meanwhile, cut the aubergines in half lengthways and gently scoop out the flesh with a small sharp knife and a spoon, leaving 5mm/¼in of the shell intact. Select a baking dish that will hold the aubergine shells snugly in a single layer. Brush it lightly with oil. Put the shells in the baking dish and chop the aubergine flesh roughly. Set aside.

3 Heat the oil in a frying pan, add the onion and cook gently, stirring frequently, until softened. Add the chopped aubergine flesh and the garlic. Cook, stirring frequently, for 6–8 minutes. Tip into a bowl and set aside. Preheat the oven to 190°C/375°F/Gas 5.

4 Drain and mash the potatoes. Add to the aubergine mixture with the ground spices and milk. Set aside 15ml/1 tbsp of the Parmesan cheese and add the rest to the aubergine mixture, stirring in salt and pepper to taste.

NUTRITIONAL NOTES

Per portion:

Energy	130Kcals/549kJ
Total fat	5g
Saturated fat	1.5g
Cholesterol	5.1mg
Fibre	3.3g

5 Spoon the mixture into the aubergine shells. Mix the breadcrumbs with the reserved Parmesan cheese and sprinkle the mixture evenly over the aubergines. Bake in the oven for 30–40 minutes until the topping is crisp. Garnish with mint sprigs and serve with salad leaves.

ITALIAN STUFFED PEPPERS

—

**This flavourful dish is easy to make for a light
and healthy lunch or supper.**

INGREDIENTS

10ml/2 tsp olive oil
1 red onion, sliced
1 courgette (zucchini), diced
115g/4oz mushrooms, sliced
1 garlic clove, crushed
400g/14oz can chopped tomatoes
15ml/1 tbsp tomato purée (paste)
25g/1oz pine nuts (optional)
30ml/2 tbsp chopped fresh basil
4 large yellow (bell) peppers
*25g/1oz/¼ cup freshly grated Parmesan
or Fontina cheese (optional)*
salt and ground black pepper
fresh basil leaves, to garnish

SERVES 4

1 Preheat the oven to 180°C/350°F/Gas 4.
Heat the oil in a pan, add the onion,
courgette, mushrooms and garlic and
cook gently for 3 minutes, stirring the
mixture occasionally.

NUTRITIONAL NOTES
Per portion:

Energy	70Kcals/293kJ
Total fat	2.5g
Saturated fat	0.4g
Cholesterol	0mg
Fibre	2.4g

2 Stir in the tomatoes and tomato purée,
then bring to the boil and simmer,
uncovered, for 10–15 minutes, stirring
occasionally, until thickened slightly.
Remove the pan from the heat and stir in
the pine nuts, if using, chopped basil and
seasoning. Set aside.

3 Cut the peppers in half lengthways and
deseed them. Blanch the pepper halves
in a pan of boiling water for about
3 minutes. Drain.

4 Place the peppers cut-side up in a
shallow ovenproof dish and fill with the
vegetable mixture.

5 Cover the dish with foil and bake in the
oven for 20 minutes. Uncover, sprinkle
each pepper half with a little grated
cheese, if using, and bake, uncovered,
for a further 5–10 minutes. Garnish with
fresh basil leaves and serve.

BAKED CHEESE POLENTA WITH TOMATO SAUCE

Polenta, or corn meal, is a staple food in Italy. It is cooked in a similar way to porridge oats, and
eaten soft, or set, cut into shapes, then cooked. Serve with crusty Italian bread.

INGREDIENTS

5ml/1 tsp salt
250g/9oz/2¹/4 cups quick-cook polenta
5ml/1 tsp paprika
2.5ml/¹/2 tsp grated nutmeg
5ml/1 tsp olive oil
1 large onion, finely chopped
2 garlic cloves, crushed
2 x 400g/14oz cans chopped tomatoes
15ml/1 tbsp tomato purée (paste)
5ml/1 tsp sugar
salt and ground black pepper
50g/2oz/¹/2 cup Gruyère cheese, grated

SERVES 6

1 Preheat the oven to 200°C/400°F/Gas 6.
Line a 28 × 18cm/11 × 7in baking tin
(pan) with clear film (plastic wrap). Bring
1 litre/1³/4 pints/4 cups water to the boil
in a pan with the salt.

2 Pour in the polenta in a steady stream and
cook for 5 minutes, stirring continuously.
Beat in the paprika and nutmeg, then
pour the mixture into the prepared tin and
smooth the surface. Leave to cool.

3 Heat the oil in a non-stick pan and
cook the onion and garlic until soft,
stirring occasionally. Stir in the tomatoes,
tomato purée, sugar and seasoning. Bring
to the boil, reduce the heat and simmer
for 20 minutes, stirring occasionally.

NUTRITIONAL NOTES
Per portion:

Energy	219Kcals/918kJ
Total fat	5g
Saturated fat	2g
Cholesterol	0mg
Fibre	1g

4 Turn the cooled polenta out on to a
chopping board, and cut evenly into
5cm/2in squares.

5 Place half the polenta squares in a
greased ovenproof dish. Spoon over half
the tomato sauce, and sprinkle half the
cheese over the top. Repeat the layers.
Bake in the oven for about 25 minutes,
until golden. Serve.

RED PEPPER RISOTTO

This delicious Italian risotto creates a flavourful and low-fat supper or main-course dish, ideally served with fresh Italian bread.

INGREDIENTS

3 large red (bell) peppers
10ml/2 tsp olive oil
3 large garlic cloves,
thinly sliced
1¹/2 x 400g/14oz cans
chopped tomatoes
2 bay leaves
1.2–1.5 litres/2–2¹/2 pints/5–6¹/4 cups
vegetable stock
450g/1lb/2¹/2 cups arborio rice or
brown rice
6 fresh basil leaves, snipped
salt and ground black pepper

SERVES 4

1 Preheat the grill (broiler) and cook the peppers until the skins are blackened and blistered all over. Put the peppers in a bowl, cover with several layers of damp absorbent kitchen paper and leave for 10 minutes. Peel off and discard the skins, then slice the peppers, discarding the cores and seeds. Set aside.

2 Heat the oil in a wide, shallow pan. Add the garlic and tomatoes and cook over a gentle heat for 5 minutes, stirring occasionally, then add the prepared pepper slices and the bay leaves. Stir well and cook gently for 15 minutes, stirring occasionally.

3 Pour the vegetable stock into a separate large, heavy pan and heat it to simmering point. Stir the rice into the vegetable mixture and cook for about 2 minutes, then add two or three ladlefuls of the hot stock. Cook, stirring occasionally, until all the stock has been absorbed into the rice.

NUTRITIONAL NOTES
Per portion:

Energy	306Kcals/1298kJ
Total fat	3.7g
Saturated fat	0.7g
Cholesterol	0mg
Fibre	2.7g

4 Continue to add stock in this way, making sure each addition has been absorbed before adding the next. When the rice is tender, season with salt and pepper. Remove the pan from the heat, cover and leave to stand for 10 minutes. Remove and discard the bay leaves, then stir in the basil. Serve.

MILANESE RISOTTO
—

This traditional Italian risotto is deliciously flavoured with garlic, shavings of Parmesan and
fresh parsley to create a filling and flavourful low-fat dish.

INGREDIENTS
2 garlic cloves, crushed
60ml/4 tbsp chopped fresh parsley
finely grated rind of
1 lemon

FOR THE RISOTTO
5ml/1 tsp (or 1 sachet) saffron threads
15g/1/2oz butter
1 large onion, finely chopped
275g/10oz/1 1/2 cups arborio rice
150ml/1/4 pint/2/3 cup dry
white wine
1 litre/1 3/4 pints/4 cups hot
vegetable stock
salt and ground black pepper
15g/1/2oz freshly shaved Parmesan cheese,
to serve

SERVES 4

3 Stir in the rice and cook it for about
2 minutes until it becomes translucent.
Add the wine and saffron mixture and
cook, stirring, for several minutes until
all the wine is absorbed.

4 Add 600ml/1 pint/2 1/2 cups of the stock
and simmer gently until the stock is
absorbed, stirring frequently.

5 Gradually add more stock, a ladleful at
a time, until the rice is tender, stirring
frequently. (The rice might be tender and
creamy before you've added all the stock,
so add it slowly towards the end.)

6 Season the risotto with salt and pepper
and transfer to a serving dish. Serve,
sprinkled with shavings of Parmesan
cheese and the garlic and parsley mixture.

NUTRITIONAL NOTES
Per portion:

Energy	258Kcals/1090kJ
Total fat	5g
Saturated fat	2.6g
Cholesterol	9.9mg
Fibre	1.3g

1 Mix together the garlic, parsley and
lemon rind in a bowl. Set aside.

2 To make the risotto, put the saffron in a
small bowl with 15ml/1 tbsp boiling water
and leave to stand. Melt the butter in a
heavy pan and gently fry the onion for
5 minutes, until softened and golden,
stirring occasionally.

RISOTTO WITH MUSHROOMS AND PARMESAN

A classic Italian risotto of mixed mushrooms, herbs and fresh Parmesan cheese, made using long grain brown rice. Serve simply, with a mixed leaf salad tossed in a fat-free dressing.

2 Stir the stock and the porcini liquid into the rice mixture. Bring to the boil, reduce the heat and simmer, uncovered, for about 20 minutes or until most of the liquid is absorbed, stirring frequently.

3 Add the porcini and fresh mushrooms, stir, and cook for a further 10–15 minutes until the rice is tender and the liquid absorbed, stirring frequently.

4 Season with salt and pepper to taste, stir in the chopped parsley and grated Parmesan and serve at once.

INGREDIENTS

10ml/2 tsp olive oil
4 shallots, finely chopped
2 garlic cloves, crushed
15g/¹/₂oz/2 tbsp dried porcini mushrooms,
soaked in 150ml/¹/₄ pint/²/₃ cup hot water
for 20 minutes
250g/9oz/1¹/₃ cups long grain brown rice
900ml/1¹/₂ pints/3³/₄ cups well-flavoured
vegetable stock
450g/1lb/6 cups mixed mushrooms, such
as closed cup, chestnut and field
(portabello) mushrooms, sliced if large
30–45ml/2–3 tbsp chopped fresh flat
leaf parsley
25g/1oz freshly grated Parmesan cheese
salt and ground black pepper

SERVES 4

1 Heat the oil in a large pan, add the shallots and garlic and cook gently for 5 minutes, stirring. Drain the porcini, reserving their liquid, and chop roughly. Set aside. Add the brown rice to the shallot mixture and stir to coat the grains in oil.

NUTRITIONAL NOTES
Per portion:

Energy	233Kcals/985kJ
Total fat	4.8g
Saturated fat	1.5g
Cholesterol	4mg
Fibre	1.9g

POTATO GNOCCHI

Gnocchi are little Italian dumplings made either with mashed potato and flour, as here, or with semolina. They should be light in texture, and must not be overworked while being made.

INGREDIENTS

1kg/2¹/4lb waxy potatoes, scrubbed
250g/9oz/2 cups plain (all-purpose) flour
1 egg
pinch of grated nutmeg
25g/1oz/2 tbsp butter
salt and ground black pepper
freshly shaved Parmesan cheese (optional)
fresh basil leaves, to garnish

SERVES 6

1 Place the unpeeled potatoes in a large pan of boiling salted water and cook until the potatoes are tender but not falling apart. Drain and peel while the potatoes are still hot.

2 On a work surface, spread out a layer of flour. Mash the hot potatoes with a food mill, dropping them on to the flour. Sprinkle with about half of the remaining flour. Mix the flour very lightly into the potatoes.

NUTRITIONAL NOTES
Per portion:

Energy	256Kcals/1083kJ
Total fat	4.6g
Saturated fat	2.4g
Cholesterol	37.8mg
Fibre	2.6g

3 Break the egg into the mixture, add the nutmeg and knead lightly, drawing in more flour as necessary. When the dough is light to the touch and no longer moist or sticky it is ready to be rolled. Do not overwork or the gnocchi will be heavy.

4 Divide the dough into four parts. On a lightly floured board, form each part into a roll about 2cm/³/4in in diameter, taking care not to overhandle the dough. Cut the rolls crossways into pieces about 2cm/³/4in long.

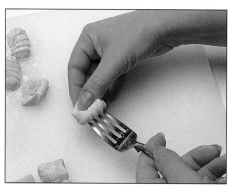

5 Hold an ordinary table fork with long tines sideways, leaning on the board. One by one, press and roll the gnocchi lightly along the tines of the fork towards the points, making ridges on one side and a depression from your thumb on the other.

6 Bring a large pan of water to a fast boil. Add salt and drop in about half the gnocchi.

7 When they rise to the surface, after 3–4 minutes, the gnocchi are done. Scoop them out, allow to drain and place in a warmed serving bowl. Dot with butter. Keep warm while the remaining gnocchi are boiling.

8 As soon as they are cooked, toss the drained gnocchi with the butter, sprinkle with a little shaved Parmesan, if using, and serve, garnished with basil and a grinding of black pepper.

VARIATION
Green gnocchi are made in exactly the same way as potato gnocchi, with the addition of fresh or frozen spinach. Use 675g/1¹/2lb fresh spinach, or 400g/14oz frozen leaf spinach. Mix with the potato and the flour in Step 2. Almost any pasta sauce is suitable for serving with gnocchi; they are particularly good with Gorgonzola sauce, or simply drizzled with a little olive oil. Gnocchi can also be served in clear soup.

PASTA WITH TOMATO AND CHILLI SAUCE

This is a speciality of Lazio. In Italian it is called *pasta all'arrabbiata* – the word *arrabbiata* means rabid or angry, and describes the heat that comes from the chilli.

INGREDIENTS

500g/1¼lb sugocasa
2 garlic cloves, crushed
150ml/¼ pint/⅔ cup dry white wine
15ml/1 tbsp sun-dried tomato purée (paste)
1 fresh red chilli
300g/11oz dried penne or tortiglioni
60ml/4 tbsp finely chopped fresh flat leaf parsley
salt and ground black pepper
15g/½oz freshly grated Pecorino cheese, to serve

SERVES 4

3 Remove the chilli from the sauce and add half the parsley. Add seasoning to taste. If you prefer a hotter taste, finely chop some or all of the chilli and return it to the sauce.

4 Drain the pasta and transfer to a warmed serving bowl. Pour the sauce over the pasta and toss to mix. Serve at once, sprinkled with a little grated Pecorino cheese and the remaining parsley.

NUTRITIONAL NOTES

Per portion:

Energy	287Kcals/1220kJ
Total fat	2.1g
Saturated fat	0.7g
Cholesterol	2.2mg
Fibre	3g

1 Put the sugocasa, garlic, wine, tomato purée and whole chilli in a pan and bring to the boil. Cover, reduce the heat and simmer gently, stirring occasionally.

2 Drop the pasta into a large pan of rapidly boiling salted water and simmer for 10–12 minutes or until tender or *al dente*.

SPAGHETTI WITH FRESH TOMATO SAUCE

This is the famous Neapolitan sauce from Italy that is made in summer when tomatoes are very ripe and sweet. Spaghetti is the traditional choice of pasta for a low-fat, flavourful Italian meal.

INGREDIENTS
675g/1¹/₂lb ripe Italian plum tomatoes
15ml/1 tbsp olive oil
1 onion, finely chopped
350g/12oz dried spaghetti
small handful of fresh basil leaves
salt and ground black pepper
15g/¹/₂oz coarsely shaved fresh Parmesan
cheese, to serve

SERVES 4

1 With a sharp knife, cut a cross in the bottom (flower) end of each tomato. Bring a medium pan of water to the boil and remove from the heat. Plunge a few of the tomatoes into the water, leave for 30 seconds or so, then lift them out with a slotted spoon. Repeat the process with the remaining tomatoes, then peel off and discard the skins and roughly chop the flesh. Set aside.

NUTRITIONAL NOTES
Per portion:

Energy	330Kcals/1399kJ
Total fat	5g
Saturated fat	1.1g
Cholesterol	2.2mg
Fibre	4.05g

2 Heat the oil in a large pan, add the onion and cook over a low heat, stirring frequently, for about 5 minutes until softened and lightly coloured. Add the tomatoes, with salt and pepper to taste. Bring to a gentle boil then cover the pan, reduce the heat and simmer for 30–40 minutes, stirring occasionally, until thick.

3 Meanwhile, cook the pasta in a large pan of boiling salted water, according to the packet instructions, until tender or *al dente*. Shred the fresh basil leaves finely.

4 Remove the sauce from the heat, stir in the basil and adjust the seasoning to taste. Drain the pasta, transfer to a warmed bowl, pour the sauce over and toss well to mix. Serve immediately, with a little shaved Parmesan handed separately.

TAGLIATELLE WITH BROCCOLI AND SPINACH

This is an excellent Italian vegetarian supper dish. It is nutritious, filling, low-fat and needs no accompaniment. If you like, you can use tagliatelle flecked with herbs.

2 Add salt to the water in the steamer and fill the steamer pan with boiling water, then add the pasta and cook, according to the packet instructions, until tender or *al dente*. Meanwhile, chop the broccoli and spinach in the colander.

INGREDIENTS

2 heads of broccoli
450g/1lb fresh spinach, stems removed
grated nutmeg, to taste
350g/12oz dried egg tagliatelle
15ml/1 tbsp extra virgin olive oil
juice of 1/2 lemon, or to taste
salt and ground black pepper
15g/1/2oz freshly grated Parmesan cheese,
to serve

SERVES 4

NUTRITIONAL NOTES
Per portion:

Energy	288Kcals/1218kJ
Total fat	4.9g
Saturated fat	1g
Cholesterol	1.9mg
Fibre	4.5g

1 Put the broccoli in the basket of a steamer, cover and steam over a pan of boiling water for 10 minutes. Add the spinach to the broccoli, cover and steam for 4–5 minutes or until both are tender. Towards the end of the cooking time, sprinkle the vegetables with freshly grated nutmeg and salt and pepper to taste. Transfer the vegetables to a colander and set aside.

3 Drain the pasta. Heat the oil in the pasta pan, add the pasta and chopped vegetables and toss over a medium heat until evenly mixed. Sprinkle in the lemon juice and plenty of black pepper, then taste and add more lemon juice, salt and nutmeg if you like. Serve immediately, sprinkled with freshly grated Parmesan and black pepper.

VARIATION
If you like, add a sprinkling of crushed dried chillies with the black pepper in Step 3.

PENNE WITH ARTICHOKES

Artichokes are a very popular vegetable in Italy, and are often used in sauces for pasta. This sauce is richly flavoured with garlic, perfect for a delicious light lunch or supper.

INGREDIENTS

juice of ¹/₂–1 lemon
2 globe artichokes
15ml/1 tbsp olive oil
1 small fennel bulb, thinly sliced, with feathery tops reserved
1 onion, finely chopped
4 garlic cloves, finely chopped
handful of fresh flat leaf parsley, roughly chopped
400g/14oz can chopped Italian plum tomatoes
150ml/¹/₄ pint/²/₃ cup dry white wine
350g/12oz/3 cups dried penne
10ml/2 tsp capers, chopped
salt and ground black pepper

SERVES 6

1 Have ready a bowl of cold water to which you have added the juice of half a lemon. Cut off the artichoke stalks, then discard the outer leaves until the pale inner leaves that are almost white at the base remain.

2 Cut off the tops of these leaves so that the base remains. Cut the base in half lengthwise, then prise the hairy choke out of the centre with the tip of the knife and discard. Cut the artichokes lengthways into 5mm/¹/₄in slices, adding them immediately to the bowl of water.

3 Bring a large pan of water to the boil. Add a good pinch of salt, then drain the artichokes and add them immediately to the water. Boil for 5 minutes, drain and set aside.

4 Heat the oil in a large frying pan or other suitable pan and add the fennel, onion, garlic and parsley. Cook over a low to medium heat, stirring frequently, for about 10 minutes until the fennel has softened and is lightly coloured.

5 Add the tomatoes and wine, with salt and pepper to taste. Bring to the boil, stirring, then cover, reduce the heat and simmer for 10–15 minutes, stirring occasionally. Stir in the artichokes, replace the lid and simmer for a further 10 minutes.

6 Meanwhile, cook the pasta in a large pan of water, according to the packet instructions. Drain, reserving a little cooking water. Stir the capers into the sauce, then adjust the seasoning and add the remaining lemon juice if you like.

7 Tip the pasta into a warmed serving bowl, pour the sauce over and mix, adding a little cooking water if necessary. Serve, garnished with fennel fronds.

NUTRITIONAL NOTES
Per portion:

Energy	269Kcals/1140kJ
Total fat	3g
Saturated fat	0.4g
Cholesterol	0mg
Fibre	2.7g

CHIFFERI RIGATE WITH AUBERGINE SAUCE

Full of flavour, this excellent Italian vegetarian sauce goes well with any short pasta shape, such
as chifferi rigati or penne, to create an appetizing lunch or supper dish.

2 Remove and discard the chilli. Add the
aubergines to the pan with the remaining
parsley and all the basil. Pour in half the
water. Crumble in the stock cube and stir
until it is dissolved, then cover and cook,
stirring frequently, for about 10 minutes.

3 Add the tomatoes, wine, sugar, saffron
and paprika, with salt and pepper to taste,
then pour in the remaining water. Stir
well, replace the lid and cook for a further
30–40 minutes, stirring occasionally.
Adjust the seasoning to taste.

4 Meanwhile, cook the pasta in a large
pan of boiling salted water, according to
the packet instructions, until tender or *al
dente*. Drain well.

5 Add the aubergine sauce to the cooked
pasta, toss together to ensure it is
thoroughly mixed and serve immediately.

INGREDIENTS
30ml/2 tbsp olive oil
1 small fresh red chilli
2 garlic cloves
2 handfuls of fresh flat leaf parsley
450g/1lb aubergines (eggplant),
roughly chopped
1 handful of fresh basil leaves
200ml/7fl oz/scant 1 cup water
1 vegetable stock (boullion) cube
8 ripe Italian plum tomatoes, skinned and
finely chopped
60ml/4 tbsp red wine
5ml/1 tsp sugar
1 sachet saffron powder
2.5ml/¹⁄₂ tsp ground paprika
450g/1lb chifferi rigati
salt and ground black pepper

SERVES 6

1 Heat the oil in a large frying pan and
add the whole chilli and whole garlic
cloves. Roughly chop the parsley and add
half to the pan. Smash the garlic cloves
with a wooden spoon to release their
juice, then cover the pan and cook the
mixture over a low to medium heat for
about 10 minutes, stirring occasionally.

NUTRITIONAL NOTES
Per portion:

Energy	300Kcals/1274kJ
Total fat	3.6g
Saturated fat	0.6g
Cholesterol	0mg
Fibre	4.1g

PENNE WITH GREEN VEGETABLE SAUCE

Lightly cooked fresh green vegetables are tossed with pasta to create this low-fat Italian dish,
ideal for a light lunch or supper.

INGREDIENTS

2 carrots
1 courgette (zucchini)
75g/3oz French (green) beans
1 small leek, washed
2 ripe Italian plum tomatoes
1 handful of fresh flat leaf parsley
15ml/1 tbsp extra virgin olive oil
2.5ml/¹/₂ tsp sugar
115g/4oz/1 cup frozen peas
350g/12oz/3 cups dried penne
salt and ground black pepper

SERVES 4

1 Dice the carrots and the courgette
finely. Trim the French beans, then cut
them into 2cm/³/₄in lengths. Slice the
leek thinly. Skin and dice the tomatoes.
Finely chop the parsley and set aside.

2 Heat the oil in a medium frying pan.
Add the carrots and leek. Sprinkle the
sugar over and cook, stirring frequently,
for about 5 minutes.

3 Stir in the courgette, French beans,
peas and plenty of salt and pepper. Cover
and cook over a low to medium heat for
5–8 minutes until the vegetables are
tender, stirring occasionally.

4 Meanwhile, cook the pasta in a large
pan of boiling salted water, according to
the packet instructions, until it is tender
or *al dente*. Drain the pasta well and keep
it hot until it is ready to serve.

5 Stir the parsley and chopped plum
tomatoes into the vegetable mixture and
adjust the seasoning to taste. Toss with
the cooked pasta and serve at once.

NUTRITIONAL NOTES
Per portion:

Energy	328Kcals/1392kJ
Total fat	4.5g
Saturated fat	0.7g
Cholesterol	0mg
Fibre	5g

BREADS, BAKES AND DESSERTS

The AROMA of freshly baked bread, to go with a meal, is hard to beat, while desserts provide the flavourful FINALE. We bring you a selection of DELECTABLE Italian breads, bakes and desserts. Choose from traditional Ciabatta and FOCACCIA breads, ZABAGLIONE and granitas for dessert, Biscotti, Chocolate AMARETTI and more.

CIABATTA

—

This irregular-shaped Italian bread is so called because it looks like an old shoe or slipper. It is made with a wet dough flavoured with olive oil, and is a great accompaniment to low-fat dishes.

INGREDIENTS
FOR THE BIGA STARTER
10g/¹⁄₄oz fresh yeast
175–200ml/6–7fl oz/scant 1 cup lukewarm water
350g/12oz/3 cups unbleached plain (all-purpose) flour, plus extra for dusting

FOR THE DOUGH
15g/¹⁄₂oz fresh yeast
400ml/14fl oz/1²⁄₃ cups lukewarm water
60ml/4 tbsp lukewarm semi-skimmed (low-fat) milk
500g/1¹⁄₄lb/5 cups unbleached strong white bread flour
10ml/2 tsp salt
45ml/3 tbsp extra virgin olive oil
MAKES 3 LOAVES, SERVES 12

1 In a small bowl, cream the yeast for the biga starter with a little of the water. Sift the flour into a bowl. Gradually mix in the yeast mixture and enough of the remaining water to form a firm dough.

2 Turn out the biga starter dough on to a lightly floured surface and knead for about 5 minutes until smooth. Return the dough to the bowl, cover with lightly oiled clear film (plastic wrap) and leave in a warm place for 12–15 hours until the dough has risen and is starting to collapse.

3 Sprinkle three baking sheets with flour and set aside. Mix the yeast for the dough with a little of the water until creamy, then mix in the remaining water. Add the yeast mixture to the biga and mix well. Mix in the milk, beating thoroughly with a wooden spoon. Mix in the flour by hand for 15 minutes, lifting the dough, to form a very wet mixture.

4 Beat in the salt and olive oil. Cover with lightly oiled clear film and leave to rise, in a warm place, for 1¹⁄₂–2 hours, or until doubled in bulk.

5 Using a spoon, tip one-third of the dough at a time on to each baking sheet, trying to avoid knocking back (punching down) the dough in the process.

6 Using floured hands, shape into oblong loaves, about 2.5cm/1in thick. Flatten slightly. Sprinkle with flour and leave to rise in a warm place for 30 minutes. Meanwhile, preheat the oven to 220°C/425°F/Gas 7. Bake the loaves for 25–30 minutes or until golden brown. Transfer to a wire rack to cool.

NUTRITIONAL NOTES
Per portion:

Energy	268Kcals/1137kJ
Total fat	3.7g
Saturated fat	0.6g
Cholesterol	0.4mg
Fibre	2.2g

OLIVE OIL BREAD ROLLS

The Italians adore interesting and elaborately shaped rolls. This distinctively flavoured bread
dough, enriched with olive oil, can be used for making rolls or shaped as one large loaf.

4 For *filoncini* (finger rolls): flatten each piece into an oval and roll to 23cm/9in without changing the shape. Make it 5cm/2in wide at one end and 10cm/4in at the other. Roll up from the wider end. Stretch to 20–23cm/8–9in long. Cut in half. Place on the baking sheets, well spaced. Lightly brush with oil, cover with oiled clear film and leave to rise, in a warm place, for 20–30 minutes.

INGREDIENTS

*450g/1lb/4 cups unbleached strong white
bread flour
10ml/2 tsp salt
15g/¹/₂oz fresh yeast
250ml/8fl oz/1 cup lukewarm water
60ml/4 tbsp extra virgin olive oil, plus
15ml/1 tbsp extra for brushing*

MAKES 16 ROLLS

1 Lightly oil three baking sheets and set aside. Sift the flour and salt together in a large bowl and make a well in the centre. In a jug, cream the yeast with half the water, then stir in the rest. Add to the well with the oil and mix to form a dough. Turn on to a lightly floured surface. Knead for 8–10 minutes until smooth and elastic. Place in an oiled bowl, cover with oiled clear film (plastic wrap) and let rise, in a warm place, for 1 hour, or until nearly doubled in bulk.

2 Turn out on to a lightly floured surface and knock back (punch down). Divide into 12 equal pieces of dough and shape into rolls as described in Steps 3, 4 and 5.

3 For *tavalli* (spiral rolls): roll each piece into a strip about 30cm/12in long and 4cm/1¹/₂in wide. Twist into a loose spiral and join the ends to make a circle. Place on the baking sheets, well spaced. Lightly brush with oil, cover with oiled clear film and leave to rise, in a warm place, for 20–30 minutes.

NUTRITIONAL NOTES
Per portion:

Energy	119Kcals/503kJ
Total fat	3.1g
Saturated fat	0.4g
Cholesterol	0mg
Fibre	0.9g

5 For *carciofi* (artichoke-shaped rolls): shape each piece into a ball and space well apart on the baking sheets. Brush with oil, cover with oiled clear film and let rise, in a warm place, for 20–30 minutes. Preheat the oven to 200°C/ 400°F/Gas 6. Using scissors, snip 5mm/¹/₄in deep cuts in a circle on the top of each roll, then five larger horizontal cuts around the sides. Bake all the rolls for 15 minutes. Transfer to a wire rack to cool. Serve warm or cold.

TUSCANY BREAD
—

This bread from Tuscany is made without salt and probably originates from the days when salt
was heavily taxed. To compensate for the lack of salt, serve with salty foods such as olives.

INGREDIENTS
500g/1¼lb/5 cups unbleached strong
white flour
350ml/12fl oz/1½ cups boiling water
15g/½oz fresh yeast
60ml/4 tbsp lukewarm water

MAKES 1 LOAF, SERVES 8

1 First make the starter. Sift 175g/6oz/
1½ cups of the flour into a large bowl.
Pour over the boiling water, leave for a
couple of minutes, then mix well. Cover
the bowl with a damp dishtowel and leave
for 10 hours.

2 Lightly flour a baking sheet and set
aside. In a bowl, cream the yeast with the
lukewarm water. Mix well into the starter.

3 Gradually add the remaining flour and
mix to form a dough. Turn out on to a
lightly floured surface and knead for
5–8 minutes until smooth and elastic.

4 Place in a lightly oiled bowl, cover with
lightly oiled clear film (plastic wrap) and
leave to rise, in a warm place, for 1–1½
hours, or until doubled in bulk.

NUTRITIONAL NOTES
Per portion:

Energy	213Kcals/906kJ
Total fat	0.8g
Saturated fat	0.1g
Cholesterol	0mg
Fibre	1.9g

5 Turn the dough out on to a lightly
floured surface, knock back (punch
down), and shape into a round.

6 Fold the sides of the round into the
centre and seal. Place seam-side up on
the prepared baking sheet. Cover with
oiled clear film and leave to rise, in a
warm place, for 30–45 minutes, or until
doubled in bulk.

7 Flatten the loaf to about half its risen
height and flip over. Cover with a large
upturned bowl and leave to rise again, in
a warm place, for 30 minutes.

8 Meanwhile, preheat the oven to
220°C/425°F/Gas 7. Slash the top of the
loaf, using a sharp knife, if wished. Bake
for 30–35 minutes, or until golden.
Transfer to a wire rack to cool. Serve in
slices or wedges.

POLENTA BREAD

Polenta is widely used in Italian cooking. Here it is combined with pine nuts to make a truly Italian bread with a fantastic flavour. Serve in slices topped with mixed salad and low-fat cheese.

INGREDIENTS
50g/2oz/¹/3 cup polenta
300ml/¹/2 pint/1¹/4 cups luke-warm water
15g/¹/2oz fresh yeast
2.5ml/¹/2 tsp clear honey
225g/8oz/2 cups unbleached strong white bread flour
25g/1oz/2 tbsp butter
30ml/2 tbsp pine nuts
7.5ml/1¹/2 tsp salt

FOR THE TOPPING
1 egg yolk
15ml/1 tbsp water
15ml/1 tbsp pine nuts (optional)

MAKES 1 LOAF, SERVES 8

1 Lightly grease a baking sheet and set aside. Mix the polenta and 250ml/8fl oz/ 1 cup of the water together in a pan and slowly bring to the boil, stirring continuously with a large wooden spoon. Reduce the heat and let simmer for 2–3 minutes, stirring occasionally. Remove from the heat and set aside to cool for 10 minutes, or until just warm.

2 In a small bowl, mix the yeast with the remaining water and honey until creamy. Sift 115g/4oz/1 cup of the flour into a large bowl. Gradually beat in the yeast mixture, then stir in the polenta mixture gradually to combine. Turn out on to a lightly floured surface and knead for 5 minutes until smooth and elastic. Cover the bowl with lightly oiled clear film (plastic wrap). Leave the dough to rise, in a warm place, for about 2 hours, or until it has doubled in bulk.

3 Meanwhile, melt the butter in a small pan, add the pine nuts and cook over a medium heat, stirring, until pale golden. Remove the pan from the heat and set aside to cool.

4 Add the remaining flour and the salt to the polenta dough and mix to form a soft dough. Knead in the pine nuts. Turn out on to a lightly floured surface and knead for 5 minutes until smooth and elastic.

5 Place in an oiled bowl, cover with clear film and leave to rise, in a warm place, for 1 hour, until doubled in bulk.

NUTRITIONAL NOTES
Per portion:

Energy	139Kcals/585kJ
Total fat	4.9g
Saturated fat	1.7g
Cholesterol	27.5mg
Fibre	0.8g

6 Knock back (punch down) the dough and turn it out on to a lightly floured surface. Cut into two equal pieces and roll each piece into a fat sausage about 38cm/15in long. Braid together and place on the baking sheet. Cover with lightly oiled clear film and leave to rise, in a warm place, for 45 minutes. Preheat the oven to 200°C/400°F/Gas 6.

7 Mix the egg yolk and water and brush over the loaf. Sprinkle with pine nuts, if using, and bake for 30 minutes, or until golden and sounding hollow. Transfer to a wire rack to cool.

SICILIAN SCROLL

A wonderful pale yellow, crusty-topped loaf, enhanced with a nutty flavour from the sesame seeds. It's perfect for serving with low-fat cheese or cooked lean meats.

INGREDIENTS

450g/1lb finely ground semolina
115g/4oz/1 cup unbleached strong white bread flour
10ml/2 tsp salt
20g/³⁄₄oz fresh yeast
360ml/12¹⁄₂ fl oz/generous 1¹⁄₂ cups lukewarm water
30ml/2 tbsp extra virgin olive oil
30ml/2 tbsp sesame seeds, for sprinkling

MAKES 1 LOAF, SERVES 8

NUTRITIONAL NOTES
Per portion:

Energy	197Kcals/833kJ
Total fat	4.1g
Saturated fat	0.6g
Cholesterol	0mg
Fibre	0.5g

1 Lightly grease a baking sheet and set aside. Mix the semolina, white bread flour and salt together in a large bowl and make a well in the centre.

2 In a jug, cream the yeast with half the water, then stir in the remaining water. Add the creamed yeast to the centre of the semolina mixture with the olive oil. Gradually incorporate the semolina and flour to form a firm dough.

3 Turn the dough out on to a lightly floured surface. Knead for 8–10 minutes until smooth and elastic. Place in a lightly oiled bowl, cover with lightly oiled clear film (plastic wrap) and leave to rise in a warm place for 1–1¹⁄₂ hours, or until the dough has doubled in bulk.

4 Turn out on to a lightly floured surface and knock back (punch down). Knead, then shape the dough into a fat roll about 50cm/20in long. Form into an "S" shape.

5 Transfer to the prepared baking sheet, cover with oiled clear film and leave to rise, in a warm place, for 30–45 minutes, or until doubled in size.

6 Meanwhile, preheat the oven to 220°C/425°F/Gas 7. Brush the top of the scroll with water and sprinkle with the sesame seeds. Bake for 10 minutes. Spray the inside of the oven with water twice during this time.

7 Reduce the oven temperature to 200°C/400°F/Gas 6 and bake for a further 25–30 minutes, or until golden. Transfer to a wire rack to cool. Serve in slices.

PROSCIUTTO LOAF

This savoury Italian bread from Parma is spiked with the local dried ham. Just a small amount
fills the loaf with marvellous flavour and creates a delicious low-fat accompaniment or snack.

INGREDIENTS
*350g/12oz/3 cups unbleached strong white
bread flour*
7.5ml/1 1/2 tsp salt
15g/1/2 oz fresh yeast
250ml/8fl oz/1 cup lukewarm water
*40g/1 1/2 oz prosciutto, torn into
small pieces*
5ml/1 tsp ground black pepper

MAKES 1 LOAF, SERVES 6

1 Lightly grease a baking sheet and set
aside. Sift the flour and salt into a bowl
and make a well in the centre. In a small
bowl, cream the yeast with 30ml/2 tbsp of
the water, then gradually mix in the rest.
Pour into the centre of the flour.

2 Gradually beat in most of the flour with
a wooden spoon to make a batter. Beat
gently at first and then more vigorously as
the batter thickens. When most of the
flour is incorporated, mix in the rest with
your hand to form a moist dough.

3 Turn out on to a lightly floured surface
and knead for 5 minutes until smooth and
elastic. Place in an oiled bowl, cover with
lightly oiled clear film (plastic wrap) and
leave to rise, in a warm place, for 1 1/2
hours, or until doubled in bulk.

4 Turn the dough out on to a lightly
floured surface, knock back (punch down)
and knead for 1 minute. Flatten to a
round, then sprinkle with half the
prosciutto and pepper. Fold in half and
repeat with the remaining ham and
pepper. Roll up, tucking in the sides.

5 Place on the prepared baking sheet,
cover with oiled clear film and leave to
rise, in a warm place, for 30 minutes.
Turn out on to a lightly floured surface,
roll into an oval, fold in half and seal the
edges. Flatten and fold again. Seal and
fold again to make a long loaf.

6 Roll into a stubby long loaf. Draw out
the edges by rolling the dough under the
palms of your hands. Place back on the
prepared baking sheet, cover with oiled
clear film and leave to rise, in a warm
place, for 45 minutes, or until the loaf has
doubled in bulk. Preheat the oven to
200°C/400°F/Gas 6.

7 Slash the top of the loaf diagonally
three or four times, using a sharp knife,
and bake in the oven for 30 minutes, or
until golden. Transfer to a wire rack to
cool. Serve in slices.

NUTRITIONAL NOTES
Per portion:

Energy	200Kcals/849kJ
Total fat	1.6g
Saturated fat	0.5g
Cholesterol	3.3mg
Fibre	1.7g

PROSCIUTTO AND PARMESAN BREAD

*This nourishing Italian bread is ideal served in slices and topped with grilled vegetables
for a tasty, low-fat lunch or supper.*

INGREDIENTS

*225g/8oz/2 cups self-raising
wholemeal (whole-wheat) flour
225g/8oz/2 cups self-raising
white flour
5ml/1 tsp baking powder
75g/3oz Prosciutto, chopped
25g/1oz/2 tbsp grated fresh
Parmesan cheese
30ml/2 tbsp chopped fresh parsley
45ml/3 tbsp Meaux mustard
350ml/12fl oz/1½ cups buttermilk
salt and ground black pepper
skimmed milk, to glaze*

MAKES 1 LOAF, SERVES 8

1 Preheat the oven to 200ºC/400ºF/Gas 6.
Flour a baking sheet, set aside. Place the
wholemeal flour in a bowl and sift in the
white flour, baking powder and 5ml/1 tsp
salt. Add 5ml/1 tsp pepper and the
prosciutto. Set aside about 15ml/1 tbsp of
the grated Parmesan and stir the rest into
the flour mixture. Stir in the parsley.
Make a well in the centre of the mixture.

2 Mix the mustard and buttermilk
together in a jug, pour into the flour
mixture and quickly mix to a soft dough.
Turn the dough out on to a lightly floured
surface and knead briefly.

3 Shape the dough into an oval loaf,
brush with milk and sprinkle with the
remaining cheese. Place the loaf on the
prepared baking sheet.

NUTRITIONAL NOTES
Per portion:

Energy	250Kcals/1053kJ
Total fat	3.65g
Saturated fat	1.30g
Cholesterol	7.09mg
Fibre	3.81g

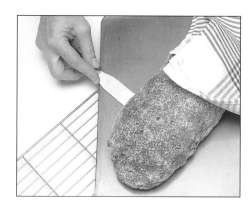

4 Bake in the oven for 25–30 minutes,
or until golden brown. Transfer to a wire
rack to cool. Serve in slices.

OLIVE AND HERB BREAD

Olive breads are popular all over the Mediterranean, especially in Italy. This delicious
olive bread is an ideal low-fat accompaniment to pasta dishes or salads.

INGREDIENTS

2 red onions, thinly sliced
30ml/2 tbsp olive oil
225g/8oz/1¹/₂ cups pitted black or
green olives
800g/1³/₄lb/7 cups strong white bread flour
7.5ml/1¹/₂ tsp salt
20ml/4 tsp easy-blend (rapid-rise)
dried yeast
45ml/3 tbsp roughly chopped fresh parsley,
coriander (cilantro) or mint
475ml/16fl oz/2 cups lukewarm water

MAKES 2 LOAVES
(EACH LOAF SERVES 10)

1 Fry the onions in the oil in a pan until
soft. Remove the pan from the heat and
set aside. Roughly chop the black or
green olives and set aside.

2 Put the flour, salt, yeast and parsley,
coriander or mint in a large bowl with the
olives and fried onions and pour in the
water. Mix to a dough using a round-
bladed knife, adding a little more water if
the mixture feels dry.

VARIATION
Shape the dough into 16 small rolls.
Slash the tops as above and reduce the
cooking time to 25 minutes.

3 Turn out on to a floured surface and
knead for about 10 minutes, until smooth
and elastic. Put in a clean bowl, cover
with clear film (plastic wrap) and leave in
a warm place until doubled in bulk.

4 Preheat the oven to 220°C/425°F/
Gas 7. Lightly grease two baking sheets.
Turn the dough out on to a lightly
floured surface and cut in half. Shape
into two rounds. Place on the prepared
baking sheets, cover loosely with lightly
oiled clear film and leave until doubled
in bulk.

5 Slash the tops of the loaves with a sharp
knife, then bake in the oven for about
40 minutes or until they sound hollow
when tapped underneath. Transfer to a
wire rack to cool. Serve in slices.

NUTRITIONAL NOTES
Per portion:

Energy	157Kcals/664kJ
Total fat	2.9g
Saturated fat	0.41g
Cholesterol	0mg
Fibre	1.8g

SAFFRON FOCACCIA

A dazzling yellow bread with a distinctive flavour, this saffron focaccia
makes a tasty snack or accompaniment.

INGREDIENTS
FOR THE DOUGH
pinch of saffron threads
150ml/¼ pint/⅔ cup boiling water
225g/8oz/2 cups plain (all-purpose) flour
2.5ml/½ tsp salt
5ml/1 tsp easy-blend (rapid-rise) dried yeast
15ml/1 tbsp olive oil

FOR THE TOPPING
2 garlic cloves, sliced
1 red onion, cut into thin wedges
fresh rosemary sprigs
*12 black olives, pitted and
coarsely chopped*
15ml/1 tbsp olive oil

MAKES 1 LOAF, SERVES 10

1 Make the dough. In a jug (pitcher),
infuse (steep) the saffron in the boiling
water. Leave until cooled to lukewarm.

2 Place the flour, salt, yeast and olive oil
in a food processor. Turn the processor on
and gradually add the saffron and its
liquid until the dough forms a ball.

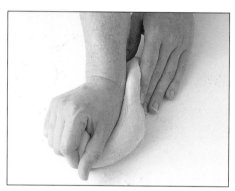

3 Transfer the dough on to a lightly
floured work surface and knead for
10–15 minutes until smooth and elastic.
Place in a bowl, cover and leave to rise in
a warm place for about 30–40 minutes,
until doubled in bulk. Lightly grease a
baking sheet and set aside.

4 Knock back (punch down) the risen
dough on a floured surface and roll out
into an oval shape about 1cm/½in thick.
Place on the baking sheet and leave to
rise in a warm place for 20–30 minutes.

5 Preheat the oven to 200°C/400°F/
Gas 6. Use your fingers to press small
indentations in the dough.

6 Cover the dough with the topping
ingredients, brush lightly with the olive
oil, and bake the loaf in the oven for
about 25 minutes or until it sounds hollow
when tapped underneath. Transfer to a
wire rack to cool. Serve the focaccia in
slices or wedges.

VARIATION
You might like to experiment with
different topping ingredients for this
bread. Green olives and sun-dried
tomatoes are two others you could try.

NUTRITIONAL NOTES
Per portion:

Energy	177Kcals/754kJ
Total fat	4.7g
Saturated fat	0.7g
Cholesterol	0mg
Fibre	1.5g

BISCOTTI

These delicious Italian biscuits are part-baked, sliced to reveal a feast of mixed nuts and then baked again until crisp and golden. They're perfect for rounding off a low-fat Italian meal.

INGREDIENTS

50g/2oz/1/4 cup unsalted (sweet) butter, softened
115g/4oz/1/2 cup caster (superfine) sugar
175g/6oz/1 1/2 cups self-raising flour
1.5ml/1/4 tsp salt
10ml/2 tsp baking powder
5ml/1 tsp ground coriander
finely grated rind of 1 lemon
50g/2oz/1/2 cup polenta
1 egg, lightly beaten
10ml/2 tsp brandy or orange liqueur
50g/2oz/1/2 cup unblanched almonds
50g/2oz/1/2 cup pistachio nuts

MAKES 24

1 Preheat the oven to 160°C/325°F/Gas 3. Lightly grease a baking sheet and set aside. Cream together the butter and sugar in a bowl.

2 Sift the flour, salt, baking powder and coriander over the creamed mixture in the bowl. Add the lemon rind, polenta, egg and brandy or liqueur and mix together to make a soft dough.

> ### COOK'S TIP
> Use a sharp, serrated knife to slice the cooled biscotti in Step 4, otherwise they will crumble.

3 Add the nuts and mix until evenly combined. Halve the mixture. Shape each half of the dough into a flat sausage about 23cm/9in long and 6cm/2 1/2in wide. Place on the prepared baking sheet. Bake in the oven for about 30 minutes until risen and just firm. Remove from the oven and set aside to cool on a wire rack.

NUTRITIONAL NOTES
Per portion:

Energy	94Kcals/397kJ
Total fat	4.2g
Saturated fat	1.2g
Cholesterol	12.6mg
Fibre	0.2g

4 When cool, cut each sausage diagonally into 12 thin slices. Return to the baking sheet and bake in the oven for a further 10 minutes until crisp.

5 Transfer the biscotti to a wire rack to cool completely. Store in an airtight container for up to one week.

CHOCOLATE AMARETTI

These mouthwatering Italian chocolate amaretti are delicious served on their own
or with low-fat ice cream, mousse or zabaglione.

INGREDIENTS

150g/5oz/1 cup blanched whole almonds
90g/3¹/₂oz/¹/₂ cup caster (superfine) sugar
15ml/1 tbsp unsweetened cocoa powder
30ml/2 tbsp icing (confectioner's) sugar
2 egg whites
pinch of cream of tartar
5ml/1 tsp almond essence (extract)
15g/¹/₂oz flaked (sliced) almonds

MAKES ABOUT 24

1 Preheat oven to 180°C/350°F/Gas 4. Place the whole almonds on a small baking sheet and bake in the oven for 10–12 minutes, stirring occasionally, until the almonds are golden brown. Remove from the oven and set aside to cool to room temperature. Reduce the oven temperature to 160°C/325°F/Gas 3.

2 Line a large baking sheet with non-stick baking parchment or foil and set aside. In a blender or food processor fitted with a metal blade, process the toasted almonds with 45g/1³/₄oz/¹/₄ cup sugar until the almonds are finely ground but not oily. Transfer to a medium bowl and sift in the cocoa powder and icing sugar; stir to mix. Set aside.

3 In a mixing bowl, beat the egg whites and cream of tartar together, using an electric mixer, until stiff peaks form. Sprinkle in the remaining 45g/1³/₄oz/ ¹/₄ cup sugar, a tablespoon at a time, beating well after each addition, and continue beating until the egg whites are glossy and stiff. Beat in the almond essence.

4 Sprinkle the almond-sugar mixture over the whisked egg whites and gently fold in until just blended. Spoon the mixture into a large piping (icing) bag fitted with a plain 1cm/¹/₂in nozzle. Pipe the mixture into 4cm/1¹/₂in rounds about 2.5cm/1in apart on the prepared baking sheet. Press a flaked almond into the centre of each one.

5 Bake the amaretti in the oven for 12–15 minutes or until they appear crisp. Place the baking sheets on a wire rack and leave to cool for 10 minutes. With a metal spatula, remove the amaretti and place on a wire rack, then leave to cool completely. When cool, store in an airtight container.

NUTRITIONAL NOTES
Per portion:

Energy	58Kcals/244kJ
Total fat	3.7g
Saturated fat	0.4g
Cholesterol	0mg
Fibre	0.6g

APRICOT AND ALMOND FINGERS

These moist apricot and almond fingers are an irresistible low-fat snack
or treat for all to enjoy.

2 Turn the mixture into the prepared tin, spread to the edges and sprinkle with the flaked almonds.

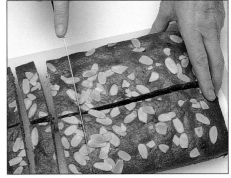

3 Bake in the oven for 30–35 minutes or until the centre of the cake springs back when lightly pressed. Turn out on to a wire rack and allow to cool. Remove and discard the paper, place the cake on a board and cut it into 18 slices with a sharp knife. Store in an airtight container.

INGREDIENTS

225g/8oz/2 cups self-raising flour
115g/4oz/⅔ cup light muscovado
(brown) sugar
50g/2oz/⅓ cup semolina
175g/6oz/1 cup ready-to-eat dried
apricots, chopped
2 eggs
30ml/2 tbsp malt extract
30ml/2 tbsp clear honey
60ml/4 tbsp skimmed milk
60ml/4 tbsp sunflower oil
few drops of almond essence (extract)
30ml/2 tbsp flaked (sliced) almonds

MAKES 18

1 Preheat the oven to 160°C/325°F/Gas 3. Lightly grease and line a 28 × 18cm/11 × 7in shallow baking tin (pan) and set aside. Sift the flour into a bowl and add the sugar, semolina, dried apricots, eggs, malt extract, honey, milk, oil and almond essence. Mix well until smooth.

NUTRITIONAL NOTES
Per portion:

Energy	153Kcals/641kJ
Total fat	4.56g
Saturated fat	0.61g
Cholesterol	21.5mg
Fibre	1.27g

ZABAGLIONE

A much-loved, simple and very delicious Italian dessert traditionally made with Marsala,
an Italian fortified wine, although Madeira is a good alternative.

INGREDIENTS

4 egg yolks
50g/2oz/¹/4 cup caster (superfine) sugar
60ml/4 tbsp Marsala or Madeira
amaretti, to serve (optional)

SERVES 6

4 Pour into six warmed, stemmed small glasses and serve immediately with the amaretti for dipping, if you like.

NUTRITIONAL NOTES
Per portion:

Energy	93Kcals/388kJ
Total fat	4.1g
Saturated fat	1.2g
Cholesterol	150.9mg
Fibre	0g

3 Now place the bowl over a pan of gently simmering water and continue to whisk for at least 5–7 minutes until the mixture becomes thick and mousse-like; when the beaters are lifted, they should leave a thick trail on the surface of the mixture.

1 Place the egg yolks and caster sugar in a large, clean, heatproof bowl and whisk with an electric beater until the mixture is pale and thick and forms fluffy peaks when the whisk is lifted out.

2 Gradually add the Marsala or Madeira, whisking well after each addition (at this stage the mixture will be quite runny).

VARIATION
If you don't have any Marsala or Madeira, you could use a medium-sweet sherry or a dessert wine.

STUFFED PEACHES WITH ALMOND LIQUEUR

Together amaretti and amaretto liqueur have an intense almond flavour, and make a natural partner for peaches in this exquisite Italian low-fat dessert.

2 Put the amaretti in a bowl and crush them finely with the end of a rolling pin. Set aside.

3 Cream the low-fat spread and sugar together in a separate bowl until smooth. Stir in the reserved chopped peach flesh, the egg yolk and half the liqueur with the amaretti crumbs. Mix well. Lightly grease an ovenproof dish that is just large enough to hold the peach halves in a single layer.

INGREDIENTS

4 ripe but firm peaches
50g/2oz/¹/₂ cup amaretti
30ml/2 tbsp low-fat spread
30ml/2 tbsp caster (superfine) sugar
1 egg yolk
60ml/4 tbsp amaretto liqueur
a little low-fat spread, for greasing
250ml/8fl oz/1 cup dry white wine
8 tiny sprigs of fresh basil, to decorate

SERVES 4

1 Preheat the oven to 180°C/350°F/Gas 4. Cut the peaches in half and remove and discard the stones (pits). With a spoon, scrape out some of the flesh from each peach half, slightly enlarging the hollow left by the stone. Chop this flesh and set it aside. Set the peach halves aside.

4 Stand the peach halves in the dish and spoon the amaretti stuffing into them. Mix the remaining liqueur with the wine, pour over the peaches and bake in the oven for 25 minutes or until the peaches feel tender. Decorate with basil sprigs and serve immediately, with a little low-fat ice cream, if you like.

NUTRITIONAL NOTES

Per portion:

Energy	232Kcals/971kJ
Total fat	5g
Saturated fat	1.37g
Cholesterol	54.7mg
Fibre	1.9g

FIGS WITH RICOTTA CREAM

Fresh, ripe figs are full of natural sweetness and need little adornment. This simple Italian recipe makes the most of their intense flavour and creates a mouthwatering low-fat dessert.

INGREDIENTS

4 ripe, fresh figs
115g/4oz/1/2 cup ricotta or cottage cheese
45ml/3 tbsp half-fat crème fraîche
15ml/1 tbsp clear honey
2.5ml/1/2 tsp vanilla essence (extract)
freshly grated nutmeg, to decorate

SERVES 4

1 Trim the stalks from the figs. Make four cuts through each fig from the stalk end, cutting them almost through but leaving them joined at the base.

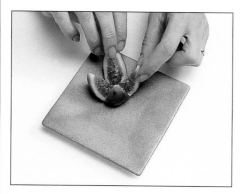

2 Place the figs on serving plates and open them out.

3 In a bowl, mix together the ricotta or cottage cheese, crème fraîche, honey and vanilla essence.

NUTRITIONAL NOTES
Per portion:

Energy	55Kcals/232kJ
Total fat	2g
Saturated fat	1.2g
Cholesterol	6.7mg
Fibre	0g

4 Spoon a little ricotta cream on to each plate and sprinkle with grated nutmeg to decorate. Serve.

ITALIAN FRUIT SALAD AND ICE CREAM

If you visit Italy in the summer, you will find little pavement fruit shops selling small dishes of macerated soft fruits, which are delectable on their own, but also wonderful with low-fat ice cream.

INGREDIENTS

900g/2lb/8 cups mixed ripe soft fruits,
such as strawberries, raspberries,
loganberries, redcurrants, blueberries,
peaches, apricots, plums and melons
juice of 6–8 oranges
juice of 1 lemon
15ml/1 tbsp pear and apple concentrate
60ml/4 tbsp very low-fat fromage frais
or mascarpone
30ml/2 tbsp orange-flavoured
liqueur (optional)
fresh mint sprigs, to decorate

SERVES 6

1 Prepare the fruit according to type. Cut it into reasonably small pieces, but not so small that the mixture becomes a mush.

2 Put the fruit in a serving bowl and pour over enough orange juice to cover. Add the lemon juice, stir gently to mix, cover and chill in the refrigerator for 2 hours.

3 Set half the macerated fruit aside to serve as it is. Purée the remainder in a blender or food processor. Pour the purée into a bowl.

4 Gently warm the pear and apple concentrate in a small pan and stir it into the fruit purée. Whip the fromage frais or mascarpone and fold it in to the fruit purée, then add the liqueur, if using.

NUTRITIONAL NOTES
Per portion:

Energy	60Kcals/254kJ
Total fat	0.2g
Saturated fat	0.01g
Cholesterol	0.1mg
Fibre	3.2g

5 Churn the mixture in an ice-cream maker. Alternatively, place in a shallow freezerproof container and freeze it until ice crystals form around the edge. Beat the mixture in a chilled bowl until smooth. Repeat the process once or twice, then freeze until firm. Soften slightly in the refrigerator before serving in scoops. Decorate with mint sprigs and serve with the macerated fruit.

LEMON GRANITA

Nothing is more refreshing on a hot summer's day than an Italian fat-free fresh lemon granita.
Try making a lime version as well.

INGREDIENTS
475ml/16fl oz/2 cups water
115g/4oz/¹/2 cup sugar
2 large lemons

SERVES 4

NUTRITIONAL NOTES
Per portion:

Energy	114Kcals/488kJ
Total fat	0g
Saturated fat	0g
Cholesterol	0mg
Fibre	0g

1 In a large pan, heat the water and the sugar together over a low heat until the sugar dissolves. Bring to the boil, stirring occasionally. Remove the pan from the heat and set aside to cool.

2 Finely grate the rind from 1 lemon, then squeeze the juice from both. Stir the grated lemon rind and juice into the sugar syrup. Pour it into a shallow plastic container or freezer tray, and freeze until it is solid.

3 Plunge the base of the frozen container or tray in very hot water for a few seconds. Turn the frozen mixture out into a bowl and chop it into large chunks.

4 Place the mixture in a blender or food processor fitted with metal blades, and process until it forms small crystals. Spoon the granita into serving glasses and serve immediately.

COFFEE GRANITA

Espresso coffee adds a delicious flavour to this appetizing fat-free Italian-style dessert.

INGREDIENTS
475ml/16fl oz/2 cups water
115g/4oz/¹/2 cup sugar
250ml/8fl oz/1 cup very strong espresso coffee, cooled

SERVES 4

1 Heat the water and sugar together in a pan until the sugar dissolves. Bring to the boil, stirring occasionally. Remove the pan from the heat and set aside to cool.

2 Stir the cooled coffee and the sugar syrup together. Pour the mixture into a shallow, plastic container and freeze until solid. Plunge the base of the frozen container in very hot water for a few seconds. Turn the frozen mixture out into a bowl and chop it into large chunks.

3 Place the mixture in a blender or food processor fitted with metal blades, and process until it forms small crystals. Spoon the granita into tall serving glasses and serve.

COOK'S TIP
If not served immediately, the granita can be frozen again.

NUTRITIONAL NOTES
Per portion:

Energy	115Kcals/488kJ
Total fat	0g
Saturated fat	0g
Cholesterol	0mg
Fibre	0g

INDEX

pork 18–19
  tagliatelle with ragù
    sauce 56
potatoes 8
  potato gnocchi 96–7
poultry 8, 18–19
prawns in fresh tomato
    sauce 66
prosciutto 18
  prosciutto and Parmesan
    bread 112
  prosciutto and pepper
    pizzas 43
  prosciutto loaf 111
  trout and prosciutto
    risotto rolls 74–5
protein foods 8, 9, 18–19

r
rabbit 18
red pepper risotto 93
rice 6, 8, 16–17
  Milanese risotto 94
  pancetta and bean
    risotto 52
  red pepper risotto 93
  risotto with mushrooms
    and Parmesan 95
  spinach and rice
    soup 32–3
  trout and prosciutto risotto
    rolls 74–5
ricotta 20
  figs with ricotta
    cream 122
roasted Mediterranean
    vegetables 88
roasted pepper and tomato
    salad 40–1
roasted plum tomatoes with

garlic 42
rocket, pear and Parmesan
    salad 36
rosemary 22

s
saffron 23
  saffron focaccia 114–5
sage 22
salami 6, 18
salt 23
saturated fats 6, 8, 9
scallops
  tagliatelle with
    scallops 78–9
seafood 19
  prawns in fresh tomato
    sauce 66
  spaghetti with squid and
    peas 78–9
  tagliatelle with
    scallops 78–9
  vermicelli with clam
    sauce 77
Sicilian scroll 110
spaghetti with fresh tomato
    sauce 99
spaghetti with meatballs 58
spaghetti with squid and
    peas 78–9
spaghetti bolognese 57
spices 23
  chicken in a salt crust 55
  monkfish with peppered
    citrus marinade 68–9
  saffron focaccia 114–5
spinach
  spinach and rice
    soup 32–3
  tagliatelle with broccoli and

spinach 100
squid
  spaghetti with squid and
    peas 78–9
stuffed aubergines 90
stuffed peaches with almond
    liqueur 121
sugar 8

t
tagliatelle with broccoli and
    spinach 100
tagliatelle: tagliatelle with
    ragù sauce 56
tagliatelle: tagliatelle with
    scallops 78–9
three-colour salad 38–9
tomatoes 11
  baked cheese polenta
    with tomato sauce 92
  baked cod with
    tomatoes 73
  beef stew with tomatoes,
    wine and peas 48
  lentil soup with
    tomatoes 32–3
  monkfish with tomato
    and olive sauce 65
  pasta with tomato and
    chilli sauce 98
  prawns in fresh
    tomato sauce 66
  roasted pepper and
    tomato salad 40–1
  roasted plum tomatoes
    with garlic 42
  spaghetti with fresh
    tomato sauce 99
  sun-dried 21
  three-colour salad 38–9

tomato and fresh basil
    soup 28
  veal with tomatoes and
    white wine 50–1
trout and prosciutto risotto
    rolls 74–5
turkey 18
  lasagne 60–1
  spaghetti bolognese 57
Tuscan chicken 54
Tuscany bread 108

v
veal with tomatoes and white
    wine 50–1
vegetables 6, 8, 9, 10–11
  baked fish with Italian
    vegetable sauce 72
  caponata 82
  minestrone 31
  penne with green
    vegetable sauce 103
  roasted Mediterranean
    vegetables 88
vermicelli with clam
    sauce 77
vitamins 8

w
weight 6, 8
wild mushroom soup 29
wine
  beef stew with tomatoes,
    wine and peas 48
  veal with tomatoes and
    white wine 50–1

z
zabaglione 120